Non-Leninist Marxism

Writings on the Workers Councils

Gorter, Pannekoek, Pankhurst, and Rühle

Red and Black Publishers, St Petersburg, Florida, 2007

Published by Red and Black Publishers, St Petersburg, Florida

First printing 2007

Publisher's Cataloging-in-Publication Data

      Non-Leninist   Marxism;   Writings   on   the   Workers Councils/Gorter, Pannekoek, Pankhurst, Rühle
    p. cm.
    ISBN 978-0-9791813-6-8
  1. Communism. 2. Socialism – Europe – History. 3. Communism – Europe – History. I. Title

HX237 .G67 2007

335.0094   LCCN 2007929495

Red and Black Publishers, PO Box 7542, St Petersburg, Florida, 33734
Contact us at: info@RedandBlackPublishers.com

Printed and manufactured in the United States of America

CONTENTS

Introduction

The framework of the worker's council was born in the turbulent upheavals in Europe between 1917 and 1920. In the wake of the Russian revolution in February 1917, a wave of radicalism swept over Europe. In Italy, the industrial workers of Turin and Genoa seized a number of factories and paralyzed the authorities with a general strike. In Germany, the government tottered on the brink of collapse, as strikes and worker uprisings came within a hair's breadth of seizing power. In Hungary, the government actually fell, and a "Soviet Government" held power for a short time. In all of these militant movements, the instrument of organization was the worker's council, an elected body of workers from each plant who organized and carried out the rebellions.

The new form of organization was seized on by militant revolutionaries as an alternative to the reformist Social Democratic parties. The Social Democrats advocated capturing the existing state through election campaigns and then legislating for government ownership of industries — their definition of "socialism". This strategy was attacked by the new council communists. "'Statifying' companies," declared Anton Pannekoek, "is not socialism; socialism is the power of the proletariat." The Italian communist Antonio Gramsci wrote that the future instruments of worker control could be seen in the worker's councils:

The socialist state already exists potentially in the institutions of social life characteristic of the exploited working class. To link these institutions, co-ordinating and ordering them into a highly centralized hierarchy of competence and powers, while respecting the necessary autonomy and articulation of each, is to create a genuine worker's democracy here and now—a worker's democracy in effective and active opposition to the bourgeois state, and prepared to replace it here and now in all its essential functions of administering and controlling the national heritage.

During the "Two Red Years" of 1919-1920, Gramsci encouraged workers in the industrial plants to transform their "workshop committees" into worker's councils that would be capable of taking over and running the plant directly and democratically.

In 1917, the Russians had deposed the Tsar and the Provisional Government by organizing into *soviets* (from the Russian word for "council"). The European council communists praised the *soviet* form of government, believing it to be based on the direct democratic control of the workplace by worker's councils. The Dutch communist Hermann Gorter pronounced, "This supple and flexible organism is the world's first socialist regime."

When word began to filter back about the Bolshevik brand of "democratic centralism", however, the council movement changed its stance toward the Russian Revolution. In 1920, when Otto Rühle toured the Soviet Union as a delegate to the Second Congress of the Communist International, he reported that the Soviets were mere tools of the ruling Bolshevik Party, and were "not councils in a revolutionary sense". Instead, he concluded, the Leninists were ruling through "bureaucracy, the deadly enemy of the council system".

A steady stream of criticism began. Pannekoek wrote, "If the most important element of the revolution consists in the masses taking their own affairs—the management of society and production—in hand themselves, then any form of organization which does not permit control and direction by the masses themselves is counter-revolutionary and harmful."

When the Bolsheviks, through the Third International, began to mold the other Communist Parties to their own image, the council movement responded with calls for democracy and rank-and-file control. Gramsci, from his prison cell in Italy, criticized the Italian

Communists, calling for "a greater intervention of the proletarian elements in the life of the party and a diminution of the powers of the bureaucracy":

> The error of the party has been to have accorded priority in an abstract fashion to the problem of party organization, which in practice has simply meant creating an apparatus of party functionaries who could be depended upon for their orthodoxy towards the official view. It was believed, and is still believed, that the revolution depends only on the existence of such an apparatus; and it is sometimes even believed that its existence can bring about the revolution.

Hermann Gorter bluntly declared, "The Russian tactics of dictatorship by party and leadership cannot possibly be correct here." Pannekoek attacked the elitist outlooks of the Leninists. "What can a small party, however principled, do when what is needed are the masses?" he asked. "And it also follows from this theory that it is not even the entire communist party that exercises dictatorship, but the Central Committee, and this it does first within the Party itself, where it takes it upon itself to expel individuals and uses shabby means to get rid of opposition." Lenin responded with a work entitled *Left-Wing Communism; An Infantile Disorder*, which attacked the council movement as "anarchist" and "undisciplined".

As the Communist Party entrenched itself more and more firmly in the Soviet Union, the attacks of the council communists became more vehement. In April 1920, Pannekoek announced, "The Executive Committee in Moscow and the leading comrades in Russia have come down completely on the side of opportunism." Pannekoek charged the Soviet Union with using the international communist movement as a tool of its own nationalistic programs:

> The Third International, as the association of communist parties preparing proletarian revolution in every country, is not formally bound by the policies of the Russian government, and it is supposed to pursue its own tasks completely independent of the latter. In practice, however, this separation does not exist; just as the Communist Party is the backbone of the Soviet Republic, the executive committee is intimately connected with the Presidium of the Soviet Republic through the persons of its members, thus forming an instrument whereby the Presidium intervenes in the politics of Western Europe. We can now see why the tactics of the Third International, laid down by congress to apply homogeneously to all capitalist countries and to be directed from

the center, are determined not only by the needs of communist agitation in those countries, but also by the political needs of Soviet Russia.

Pannekoek's fears were confirmed after the rise of Stalin and the subsequent flip-flops of the Comintern program. Before the outbreak of World War II, after Stalin signed a Non-Aggression Pact with Hitler, the Communist Parties were instructed to intensify the fight against the Social Democratic parties in Europe, who were to be considered as being objectively no different from the fascists — "social-fascists". As soon as Hitler invaded Russia, however, this tune abruptly changed: now the Communist Parties were instructed to form coalitions with the Social Democrats as part of a "united front of anti-fascist forces". "The politics of Lenin," Pannekoek concluded, "had their logical culmination in Stalinism in Russia."

Karl Korsch also fought against the domination of the Comintern by the USSR, remarking in disgust that the international movement had been reduced to "the one 'Marxist-Leninist' doctrine which alone brings salvation." Gorter wrote, "If the Russian tactics are still pursued here after all the disastrous consequences that they have already had here, then it will no longer be stupidity, but a crime; a crime against the revolution."

In 1921, when the sailors at the Kronstadt Fortress mutinied in an attempt to overthrow the Communist Party and re-institute the Soviet government and direct worker control, the council communists cheered them on. "Now that the proletariat in Kronstadt has risen up against you, the communist party," Gorter wrote, "now that you have had to declare a state of emergency in Petrograd against the proletariat . . . has the thought still not occurred to you, even now, that dictatorship by the proletariat is really preferable to dictatorship by the party?" Gorter concluded:

> Your real fault, which neither we nor history can forgive, is to have foisted a counter-revolutionary program and tactics upon the world proletariat, and to have rejected the really revolutionary ones which could have saved us.

The protests of the council movement were in vain, however. The Bolsheviks succeeded in imposing a program of "21 Points" upon the Comintern parties that effectively made them instruments of Stalin's Central Committee. The "left-wing" council communists were expelled from the party, and most went into exile and obscurity. The ruling Bolsheviks removed the last vestiges of the *soviet* government, crushed rank-and-file rebellions led by the Kronstadt sailors and by the Ukrainian councilist Nestor Makhno, and expelled and purged the councilist "Worker Opposition" within the Communist Party government. In essence, the Bolsheviks installed "socialism" by destroying socialism. By 1925, the council communist movement had all but ceased to exist.

By 1991, however, the council communists had been vindicated—Leninism had proven itself to be bankrupt and discredited. Leninist regimes in the USSR and Eastern Europe collapsed, and those in China, Cuba and North Korea were increasingly isolated, irrelevant, and seemed to be on the verge of doing the same.

This volume is a collection of writings from the council communists. After the collapse of Leninism in the former Soviet Empire, these writings are more relevant than ever. Leninism, in all of its various forms, cannot serve as a model for a successful anti-capitalist revolution—and Leninism in all its forms needs to be opposed by working class militants to the same extent as the capitalists.

It is my hope that, by rejecting Leninists and Leninism, the working class movement can return to its roots and transform socialism from a regimented work camp into a society with freedom and democracy *within* the workplace as well as outside it.

Editor, Red and Black Publishers
St Petersburg, Florida, 2007

PART ONE
Hermann Gorter

Open Letter to Comrade Lenin

Workers' Dreadnaught, London, 12 March-11 June 1921

I Introduction

Dear Comrade Lenin,

I have read your brochure on the Radicalism in the Communist movement. It has taught me a great deal, as all your writings have done. For this I feel grateful to you, and doubtless many other comrades feel as I do. Many a trace, and many a germ of this infantile disease, to which without a doubt, I also am a victim, has been chased away by your brochure, or will yet be eradicated by it. Your observations about the confusion that revolution has caused in many brains, is quite right too. I know that. The revolution came so suddenly, and in a way so utterly different from what we expected. Your words will be an incentive to me, once again, and to an even greater extent than before, to base my judgment in all matters of tactics, also in the revolution, exclusively on reality, on the actual class-relations, as they manifest themselves politically and economically.

After having read your brochure I thought all this is right.

But after having considered for a long time whether I would cease to uphold this "Left Wing," and to write articles for the KAPD and the Opposition party in England, I had to decline.

Basis Mistaken.

This seems contradictory. It is due, though, to the fact that the starting-point in the brochure is not right. To my idea you are mistaken in your judgment regarding the analogy of the West-European revolution with the Russian one, regarding the conditions of the West-European revolution, that is to say the class-relations, and this leads you to mistake the cause, from which this Left Wing, the opposition, originates.

Therefore the brochure *seems* to be right, as long as your starting-point is assumed. If, however (as it should be), your starting point is rejected, the entire brochure is wrong. As all your mistaken, and partly mistaken, judgments converge in your condemnation of the Left movement, especially in Germany and England, and as I firmly intend to defend those of the Left Wing, although, as the leaders know, I do not agree with them on all points, I imagine I had best answer your brochure by a defense of the Left Wing. This will enable me not only to point out its origin (the cause from which it springs), and to prove its right, and merits, in the present stage, and here, in Western Europe, but also, which is of equal importance, to combat the mistaken conceptions that are prevalent in Russia with regard to the West-European Revolution.

Both these points are of importance, as it is on the conception of the West-European revolution that the West-European as well as the Russian tactics depend. I should have liked to do this at the Moscow Congress, which, however, I was not able to attend.

Two Arguments Refuted.

In the first place I must refute two of your arguments, that may mislead the judgment of comrades or readers. You scoff and sneer at the ridiculous and childish nonsense of the struggle in Germany, at the "dictatorship of the leaders or of the masses," at "from above or below," etc. We quite agree with you, that these should be no questions at all. But we do not agree with your scoffing. For that is the pity of it: in Western- Europe they still are questions. In Western Europe we still have, in many countries, leaders of the type of the Second International; here we are still seeking the right leaders, those that do not try to dominate the masses, that do not betray them; and as long as we do not find these leaders, we want to do all things from below, and through the dictatorship of the masses themselves. If I have a mountain-guide, and he should lead me into the abyss, I prefer to do without him. As soon as we have found the right guides, we will stop this searching. Then mass and leader will be really one. This, and nothing else, is what the German and English Left Wing, what we ourselves, mean by these words.

And the same holds good for your second remark, that the leader should form one united whole with class and mass. We quite agree with you. But the question is to find and rear leaders that are really one with the masses. This can only be accomplished by the masses, the political parties and the Trade Unions, by means of the most severe struggle, also inwardly. And the same holds good for iron discipline, and strong centralisation. We want them all right, but not until we have the right leaders. This severest of all struggles, which is now being fought most strenuously in Germany and England, the two countries where Communism is nearest to its realisation, can only be harmed by your scoffing. Your attitude panders to the opportunist elements in the Third International. By this scoffing, you abet the opportunist elements in the Third International.

For it is one of the means by which elements in the Spartakus League and in the BSP, and also in the Communist Parties in many other countries, imposes upon the workers, when they say that the entire question of masses and leader is absurd, is "nonsense and childishness." Through this phrase they avoid, and wish to avoid, all criticism of themselves, the leaders. It is by means of this phrase of an iron discipline and centralisation, that they crush the opposition. And this opportunism is abetted by you.

You should not do this, Comrade. We are only in the introductory stage yet, here in Western Europe. And in that stage it is better to encourage the fighters than the rulers.

I only touch on this quite perfunctorily here. In the course of this writing I will deal with this matter more at length. There is a deeper reason yet why I cannot agree with your brochure. It is the following

Difference Between Russia and W. Europe.

On reading your pamphlets, brochures and books, nearly all of which writings filled us with admiration and approbation, we Marxists of Western Europe invariably came to a point where we suddenly grew wary, and on the look-out for a more detailed explanation; and if we failed to find this explanation, we accepted the statement but grudgingly, with all due reservations. This was your statement regarding the workers and the poor peasants. It occurs often, very often. And you always mention both these categories as revolutionary factors all the world over. And nowhere, at least as far as I have read, is there a clear and outspoken recognition of the immense difference which prevails in the matter between Russia (and a few other countries in Eastern Europe) and Western Europe (that is to say Germany, France, England, Belgium, Holland, Switzerland, and the Scandinavian countries, and perhaps even Italy). And yet, in my opinion, the fundamental difference between your conception of the tactics concerning Trade Unionism and Parliamentarism, and that of the so-called Left Wing in Western Europe, lies mainly in this point.

Of course you know this difference as well as I do, only you failed to draw from it the conclusions for the tactics in Western Europe, at least as far as I am able to judge from your works. These conclusions you have not taken into consideration, and consequently your judgment on these West-European tactics is false.(1)

And this is all the more dangerous, because this phrase of yours is parroted automatically in all the Communist Parties of Western Europe, even by Marxists. To judge from all Communist papers, magazines and brochures, and from all public assemblies, one might even surmise that a revolt of the poor peasants in Western

Europe might break out at any moment! Nowhere is the great

---

1. In *State and Revolution*, for instance, you write (page 67): "The greatest majority of the peasantry in every capitalist country that has any peasantry at all, is oppressed by the government, and so thirsting for the latter's overthrow, for 'cheap' government. The proletariat is called upon to carry this into execution . . ." The trouble is, however, that the peasantry does not thirst for Communism.

difference with Russia pointed out, and thus the judgment, also of the proletariat, is led astray. Because in Russia you were able to triumph with the help of a large class of poor peasants, you represent things in such a way, as if we in Western Europe are also going to have that help. Because you, in Russia, have triumphed exclusively through this help, you wish to make us believe that here also we will triumph through this help. You do this by means of your silence with regard to this question, as it stands in Western Europe, and your entire tactics are based on this representation.

Poor Peasants Decisive Factor.

This representation, however, is not the truth. There is an enormous difference between Russia and Western Europe. In general the importance of the poor peasants as a revolutionary factor decreases from east to west. In some Parts of Asia, China, and India, in the event of a revolution, this class would be the absolutely decisive factor; in Russia it constitutes an indispensable and, indeed, one of the main factors; in Poland, and in a few states of South-Eastern and Central Europe, it is still of importance for the revolution, but further West its attitude grows ever more antagonistic towards the revolution.

Russia had an industrial proletariat of some seven or eight millions. The number of poor peasants, however, amounted to about 25 millions. (I beg you to excuse the inevitable numerical errors; I have to quote from memory, as this letter should be despatched with all speed). When Kerensky failed to give these poor peasants the soil, you knew that before long they would come to you, the minute they should become aware of the fact. This is not so in Western Europe, and will not become so either; in the countries of Western Europe, which I have named, conditions of that sort do not exist.

The poor peasant here lives under conditions quite different from those of Russia. Though often terrible, they are not as appalling as they were there. As farmers or owners, the poor peasants possess a piece of land. The excellent means of transport enables them often to sell their goods. At the very worst they can mostly provide their own food. During the last ten years things have improved somewhat for them. Now, during and since the war, they can obtain high prices. They are indispensable, the import of foodstuffs being very limited. Regularly, therefore, they will be able to get high prices. They are supported by Capitalism. Capitalism will maintain them, as long as it can maintain itself. In your country, the position of the poor peasants was far more terrible. With you, therefore, the poor peasants had a political, revolutionary programme, and were organised in a political, revolutionary party: with the social-revolutionaries. With us this is nowhere the case. Moreover, in Russia there was an enormous amount of landed property to be divided, large estates, crown lands, government land, and the estates held by the monasteries. But the Communists of Western Europe, what can they offer to the poor peasants, to win them to their side?

Nothing to Offer Peasants.

Germany counted, before the war, from four to five million poor peasants (up to two hectares). Only eight or nine millions, however, were employed in actual large-scale industries (over 100 hectares). If the Communists were to divide all of these, the poor peasants would still be poor peasants, as the seven or eight million field-labourers also claim their share. And they cannot even divide them, as they will use them as large-scale industries. (2)

These numbers show that in Western Europe there are comparatively few poor peasants; that, therefore, the auxiliary forces, if there were any at all, would be very few in numbers.

The Communists in Germany, therefore, except in relatively insignificant regions, do not even have the means to win over the poor peasants. For the medium and small industries will surely not be expropriated. And it is practically the same in the case of the four or five million poor peasants in France, and also for Switzerland, Belgium, Holland, and two of the Scandinavian countries. (3) Everywhere small and medium sized industry prevails. And even in Italy there is no absolute certainty; not to mention England, which counts only some one or two hundred thousand peasants.

Neither will they be attracted by the promise that under Communism they will be exempt from rent-paying and mortgage-rent. For with Communism they see the approach of civil war, the

---

2. The Agrarian Theses of Moscow acknowledges this.

3. I have no statistical data for Sweden and Spain.

---

loss of markets, and general destruction.

Unless, therefore, there should come a crisis far more terrible than the present one in Germany, a crisis, indeed, far exceeding the horrors of any other crises that ever were before, the poor peasants in Western Europe will side with Capitalism, as long as it has any life left. **(4)**

Industrial Workers Stand Alone.

The workers in Western Europe stand all alone. Only a very slight portion of the lower middle class will help them. And these are economically insignificant. The workers will have to make the revolution all by themselves. Here is the great difference as compared to Russia.

Possibly you will say, Comrade Lenin, that this was the case in Russia. There also the proletariat has made the revolution all by itself. It is only after the revolution that the poor peasants joined. You are right, and yet the difference is immense.

You knew with absolute certainty that the peasants would come to you, and that they would come quickly. You knew that Kerensky would not, and could not give them the land. You knew that they would not help Kerensky long. You had a magic charm, "The Land to the Peasants," by means of which you would win them in the course of a few months to the side of the proletariat. We, on the other hand, are certain that for some time to come the poor peasants, all over Western Europe, will side with Capitalism.

You will possibly say that, although in Germany there is no great mass of poor peasants whose assistance can be relied on, the millions of proletarians that side as yet with the bourgeoisie are sure to come round. That, therefore, the place of the poor peasants in Russia will here be taken by the proletarians, so that there is help all

---

4. In the brochure, *The World Revolution*, I have emphatically pointed out this difference between Russia and Western Europe. The development of the German Revolution has proved that any judgment was even too optimistic. In Italy it is possible that the poor peasants will side with the proletariat.

the same. This representation is also fundamentally wrong, and the immense difference remains.

The Russian peasants joined the proletariat *after* Capitalism has been defeated; but when the German workers that are now as yet on the side of Capitalism join the ranks of the Communists, the struggle against Capitalism will begin in real earnest.

The revolution in Russia was terrible for the proletariat in the long years of its development and it is terrible now, after the victory. But at the actual time of revolution it was easy, and this was due to the peasants.

With us it is quite the contrary. In its development the revolution was easy, and it will be easy afterwards; but its actual coming will be terrible – more terrible, perhaps, than any other revolution ever was, for Capitalism, which in your country was weak and only slightly rooted as it were to feudalism, the middle ages and even barbarism, here in our country is strong and widely organised and deeply rooted, and the lower middle classes as well as the peasants, who always side with the strongest, with the exception of a shallow and economically unimportant layer, will stand with Capitalism until the very end.

The revolution in Russia was victorious with the help of the poor peasants. This should always be borne in mind here in Western Europe and all the world over. But the workers in Western Europe stand alone: this should never be forgotten in Russia.

The proletariat in Western Europe stands alone.

This is the absolute truth: and on this truth our tactics must be based. All tactics that are not based on this are false, and lead the proletariat to terrible defeat.

Practice also has proved that these assertions are true, for the poor peasants in Western Europe have not only no programme and failed to claim the land, but they do not even stir now that Communism is approaching. As I have observed before, this statement is not to be taken absolutely literally. There are regions in Western Europe where, as we have mentioned before, landed property on a large scale is predominant, and where the peasants are therefore in favour of Communism. There are yet other regions where the local conditions are such that the poor peasants may be won for Communism. But these regions are comparatively small. Neither do I wish to imply that quite at the close of the revolution, when all things are coming down, there will be no poor peasants doming to our side. They undoubtedly will. That is why we must carry on an unceasing propaganda amongst them. Our tactics, however, must be adopted for the beginning and for the course of the revolution. What I mean is the general trend, the general tendency of conditions. And it is on these alone that our tactics must be based. **(5)**

From this there follows in the first place – and it should be clearly, emphatically and plainly stated – that in Western Europe the real revolution, that is to say the overthrow of Capitalism, and the erection and permanent institution of Communism, for the time being is possible only in those countries where the proletariat *by itself* is strong enough against all the other classes – in Germany, England, and Italy, where the help of the poor peasants is not possible. In the other countries the revolution can only be prepared as yet by means of propaganda, organisation and fighting. The revolution itself can only follow when the economic conditions will be thus much shaken through the revolution in the big States (Russia, Germany, and England), that the bourgeois class will have grown sufficiently weak. For you will agree with me that we cannot base our tactics on events that may dome, but that may also never happen (help from the Russian armies, risings in India, terrible crises, etc., etc.).

That you should have failed to recognise this truth concerning the importance of the poor peasants, Comrade, is your first great mistake, and likewise that of the Executive in Moscow and of the International Congress.

What does it mean with regard to tactics, this fact that the proletariat of Western Europe stands all alone: that it has no prospect of any help whatsoever from any other class?

It means, in the first place, that the demands made on the masses are far greater here than in Russia – that, therefore, the proletarian mass is of far greater importance in the revolution. And in the second place that the importance of the leaders is

---

5. You, Comrade, will surely not try and win in an argument by taking the assertions of your opponent in too absolute a sense, as small minds do. My above remark, therefore, is meant for the latter.

---

proportionately smaller.

For the Russian masses, the proletarians, knew for certain, and already saw during the war, and in part before their very eyes, that the peasants would soon be on their side. The German proletarians, to take them first, know that they will be opposed by German Capitalism in its entirety, with all its classes.

It is true that already before the war the German proletarians numbered from nineteen to twenty million actual workers, of a population of seventy million, but they stood alone against all the other classes. (6) They are opposed by a Capitalism that is immeasurably stronger than that of Russia – and they are *unarmed*. The Russians were armed.

From every German proletarian therefore, from every individual, the revolution demands a far greater courage and spirit of sacrifice than was necessary in Russia.

This is the outcome of the economic class relations in Germany, and not of some theory or idea risen from the brain of revolutionary romantics or intellectuals!

Unless the entire class or at least the great majority stand up for the revolution personally, with almost superhuman force, in opposition to all the other classes, the revolution will fail; for you will agree with me again that on determining our tactics we should reckon with our own forces, not with those from outside – on Russian help, for instance.

The proletariat almost unarmed, alone, without help, against a closely united Capitalism, means for Germany that every proletarian must be a conscious fighter, every proletarian a hero; and it is the same for all Western Europe.

For the majority of the proletariat to turn into conscious, steadfast fighters, into real Communists, they must be greater, immeasurably greater, here than in Russia, in an absolute as well as a relative sense. And once more: this is the outcome, not of the representations, the dreams of some intellectual, or poet, but of the purest realities.

---

6. Of course I had to take the pre-war figures, and have made the increase in proletarians after the last census (of 1909) proportionate to that before.

And as the importance of the class grows, the importance of the leaders becomes relatively less. This does not mean that we must not have the very best of leaders. The best are not good enough; we are trying hard to find them. It only means that the importance of the leaders, as compared to that of the masses, is decreasing.

For you, who had to win a country of 160 million, with the help of seven or eight million, the importance of the leaders was certainly immense! To triumph over so many, with so few, is in the first place a matter of tactics. To do as you did, Comrade, to win such a huge land, with such small forces, but with assistance from outside, all depends in the first place on the tactics of the leader. When you, Comrade Lenin, started the struggle with a small gathering of proletarians, it was in the first place your tactics that in the crucial moments waged the battles and won the poor peasants.

But what about Germany? There the cleverest of tactics, the greatest clarity, even the genius of leaders, cannot attain much. There you have an inexorable class enmity, one against all the others. There the proletarian class must tip the scales for itself – through its power, its numbers. Its power, however, is based above all on its quality, the enemy being so mighty and so endlessly better organised and armed than the proletariat.

You opposed the Russian possessing classes, as David opposed Goliath. David was little, but he had a deadly weapon. The German, the English, the West-European proletariat oppose Capitalism as one giant does another. Between them all depends on strength – strength of body, and above all of mind.

Have you not observed, Comrade Lenin, that in Germany there are no great leaders? They are all quite ordinary men. This points to the fact that this revolution must in the first place be the work of the masses, not of the leaders.

To my idea this is something more wonderful and grand than has ever been, and it is an indication of what Communism will be.

And as it is in Germany, it is in all Western Europe, for everywhere the proletariat stands alone.

The revolution of the masses, of the workers – of the masses of workers alone, for the first time in the world.

And not because thus it is good, or beautiful, or conceived in someone's brain, but because the economic and class relations will it. (7)

In other words, and to read the matter as clearly as possible: the relation between the West-European and the Russian revolution can be demonstrated by means of the following comparison:

Supposing that in an Asiatic country like China or British India, where only one half a per cent of the inhabitants are industrial proletarians, and 80 per cent small peasants, a revolution should break out, and should be successfully carried through by those small peasants under the lead of the politically and socially more trained proletarians that were united in local trade unions and co-operatives. If these Chinese or Indian workers proclaimed to them:

"We have won through our local trade unions and co-operatives, and now you must do the same with regard to your revolution," what would the Russian workers have replied? They would have said:

"Dear friends, this is impossible. Our country is far more developed than yours. With us not half, but three per cent of the population are industrial proletarians. Our Capitalism is more powerful than yours, therefore we need better and more powerful organisations than you did."

From this difference between Russia and Western Europe there follows likewise:

1. That when you, or the Executive in Moscow, or the opportunist Communists of Western Europe, of the Spartakus League, or of the English Communist Party, say: "It is nonsense to fight about the question of leader or masses," that you in that case are wrong as regards us, not only because we are yet trying to find those leaders, but also because for you this question has quite another meaning.

2. That when you say to us: "Leader and mass must be one inseparable whole," you are wrong, not only because we are striving

---

7. I do not touch here on the fact that through this other relation of numbers (20 million to 70 million in Germany!) the importance of the mass and the leaders, and the relation between mass, party and leaders, also in the course and at the close of the revolution here, will differ from those of Russia.

for that unity, but also because that question has another meaning for you than for us.

3. That when you say: "In the Communist Party there should reign iron discipline, and absolute military centralisation," this is wrong, not only because we are seeking iron discipline and strong centralisation, but also because this question has a different meaning for us and for you.

4. That when you say: "We acted in such and such a way in Russia (after the Kornilov offensive for instance, or some other episode), or entered Parliament during this or that period, or we remained in the trade unions, and therefore the German proletariat must do the same," all this means absolutely nothing, and need not or cannot be applicable in any way. For the West-European class relations in the struggle, in the revolution, are quite different from those of Russia.

5. That when you wish to force upon us tactics that were good in Russia – tactics, for instance, that were based, consciously or unconsciously, on the conviction that here the poor peasants will soon join the proletariat – in other words, that the proletariat does not stand alone – that your tactics, which you prescribe, and which are followed here, will lead the West-European proletariat into ruin, and the most terrible defeat.

6. That when you, or the Executive in Moscow, or the opportunist elements in Western Europe, like the Central Board of the Spartakus League or the BSP, try to compel us to follow opportunist tactics (opportunism always seeks the support of outside elements, that forsake the proletariat), you are wrong.

The general bases on which the tactics in Western Europe must be founded are these: the recognition that the proletariat stands alone, that it is to expect no help, that the importance of the mass is greater, and that of the leaders relatively smaller.

This was not seen by Radek when he was in Germany, not by the Executive in Moscow, nor by you, as is evident from your words.

And it is on these bases that the tactics of the Kommunistische-Arbeiter Partei in Germany, the Communist Party of Sylvia Pankhurst (8), and the majority of the Amsterdam Commission, as appointed by Moscow, are founded.

---

8. So far, at least.

It is on these grounds that they strive, above all, to raise the masses as a whole, and the individuals to a higher level, to educate them one by one to be revolutionary fighters, by making them realise (not through theory only, but especially by practice), that all depends on them, that they are to expect nothing from foreign help, very little from leaders, and all from themselves.

Theoretically, therefore, and apart from private utterances, minor questions and excrescences, which like those of Wolffheim and Laufenberg, are inevitable in the first phases of a movement, the view taken by these parties and comrades is quite right, and your opposition absolutely wrong. (9)

On going from the East to the West of Europe, we traverse at a given moment an economic boundary. It runs from the Baltic to the Mediterranean, somewhere from Danzig to Venice. This line divides two worlds. West of this line there is a practically absolute domination of industrial, commercial and financial capital, united in the most highly developed banking capital.

Even agricultural capital is subject to, or has been compelled to unite with, this capital. This capital is organised to the utmost degree, and converges in the most firmly established State Governments of the world.

East of the line there is neither this gigantic development of industrial, commercial, transport and banking capital, not its almost absolute domination, nor, consequently, the firmly established modern State.

It would be marvellous, indeed, if the tactics of the revolutionary proletariat west of this boundary-line were the same as in the east!

II. The Question of the Trade Unions

Having brought forward the general theoretical bases, I will now proceed to prove, also by practice, that the Left Wing in Germany and England is right in general principles – on the questions of the Trade Unions and of parliamentarism.

9. It has struck me that in this controversy you almost invariably make use of private, and not public voices of the opposition.

First we will take the question of the Trade Unions.

As parliamentarism embodies the spiritual, thus the Trade Union movement embodies the material power of the leaders over the masses of the workers. Under capitalism the Trade Unions constitute the natural organisations for uniting the proletariat, and as such Marx, already from the very beginning, has demonstrated their importance. Under a more developed capitalism, and to a greater extent even in the age of imperialism, the Trade Unions have ever more become gigantic unions, with a trend of development, equal to that of the bourgeois State bodies themselves. They have produced a class of officials, a bureaucracy, that controls all the engines of power of the organisation, the finances, the press, the appointment of lower officials; often it is invested with even greater power, so that from a servant of the rank and file, it has become the master, identifying itself with the organisation. The Trade Unions can be compared to the State and its bureaucracy, also in this: that, notwithstanding the democracy that is supposed to reign there, the members are unable to enforce their will against the bureaucracy; every revolt is broken against the cleverly constructed apparatus of official ordinances and statutes, before it has been able even to shake the highest regions.

Only the most tenacious perseverance over several years can obtain even a moderate result, which mostly remains restricted to a change of persons. In the last few years, before and after the war, in England, Germany, and America, this often gave rise to rebellions of the members, who started strikes on their own account, against the will of the leaders, or the decrees of the union itself. That this should seem natural, and be accepted as such, is an indication in itself that the organisation does not represent the totality of the members, but something altogether foreign to them; and the workers do not control their union, but that the union is placed over them as an outside power against which they can rebel – a power which, all the same, has its origin in themselves: again, therefore, an analogy with the State. Once the revolt is over, the old domination begins again. In spite of the hatred and impotent exasperation of the masses, this domination manages to maintain itself, owing to the indifference and lack of clear insight, and of a united, indomitable will in the masses, and upheld as it is by the inner need for the Trade Unions, the only means the workers have to gain strength through unity, in their struggle against capital.

Warning of TU Influence

Fighting against capital, in a constant opposition against its tendency of increasing misery, and enabling the working class, through the restriction of these tendencies, to keep the existence the Trade Union movement, has played its part under capitalism, and has thus become itself a member of capitalist society. It is only at the beginning of the revolution, when the proletariat, from a member of capitalist society, is turned into the annihilator of this society, that the Trade Union finds itself in opposition to the proletariat.

That which Marx and Lenin demonstrated for the State: that its organisation, in spite of formal democracy, makes it impossible to turn it into an Instrument of the proletarian revolution, must also hold good therefore for the Trade Union organisations. Their counter-revolutionary power cannot be destroyed or weakened through a change of staff, through the replacing of reactionary leaders by radical or revolutionary elements.

It is the form of organisation that renders the masses as good as powerless, and prevents them from turning the Trade Unions into the organs of their will. The revolution can triumph only if it completely destroys this organisation: that is to say, if it alters the form of organisation so fundamentally as to turn it into something altogether different. The Soviet system, the construction from within, is not only able to uproot and abolish the State, but also the Trade Union bureaucracy: it will constitute not only the new political organs of the proletariat as opposed to capitalism, but likewise the foundation for the new Trade Unions. In the party factions in Germany, the idea of a form of organisation being revolutionary has been mocked at, because it is only the revolutionary sentiment, the revolutionary mind of the members, that matters. However, if the most important part of the revolution consists in the masses conducting their own concerns – the control of society and production – then every form of organisation that does not allow the masses to rule and to guide for themselves, must needs be counter-revolutionary and harmful, and as such it must be replaced by another form, which is revolutionary in so far as it allows the workers to decide matters for themselves.

Through their very nature the Trade Unions are useless arms for the West-European revolution! Apart from the fact that they have become tools of capitalism, and that they are in the hands of traitors, apart from the fact that through their nature they are bound to make slaves of the members, no matter what the leaders may be, they are also unfit for use generally.

The Harder Task of Europe.

The Trade Unions are too weak in the contest against the most highly-organised capital in Western-European States. These latter are powerful: the unions are not. To a great extent the Trade Unions are Professional Unions as yet, which cannot make a revolution, if it were for that fact alone. And in so far as they are industrial unions, they are not founded on the factories, on the workshops themselves, and are consequently weak. Also they are more unions for mutual aid than for struggle, dating as they do from the days of the small bourgeoisie. Even before the revolution, their organisation was already inadequate for the struggle; for the Revolution itself it cannot serve at all – in Western Europe. For the factories, the workers in the factories, make the revolution, not in the industries and professions, but in the workshops. Moreover, these unions are far too slow-working, complicated instruments, good only for the evolutionary period. Even if the revolution should not succeed right away, and we had once more to revert to peaceful action for a while, the Trade Unions would have to be destroyed and replaced by industrial unions, on a basis of industrial or workshop organisation. And with these miserable Trade Unions, that must be done away with in any case, they want to make the revolution! The workers in Western Europe need *weapons* for the revolution. The only weapons for the revolution in Western Europe are Industrial Organisations. And these united into *one* big whole!

The workers in Western Europe need the very best weapons. They stand alone: they have no help. And therefore they need these industrial organisations. In Germany and England they need them at once, because there the revolution is nearest at hand. The other countries must have them as soon as possible, as soon as we can build them.

It is no good at all, Comrade Lenin, your saying: in Russia we did it in such and such a way, for in the first place you had no organisations that were so inadequate for the struggle as many of the Trade Unions are here. You had industrial unions. Secondly, your workers were more revolutionary in spirit. Thirdly, the organisation of the capitalists was weak: and the State also. And in the fourth place, and this is the main point: you had help. You did not need the very best of weapons. We stand alone, we must have them. We will not win unless we have them. We will be defeated over and over again, unless we have them.

Other grounds than material ones also demonstrate this.

Recall in your mind, Comrade, how things were in Germany, before and during the war. The Trade Unions, the far too weak but only means, were entirely in the hands of the leaders, who used them as dead machines on behalf of capitalism. Then the revolution broke out. The Trade Unions were used by the leaders and the masses of members as a weapon against the revolution. It was through their help, through their cooperation, through their leaders, nay, partly even through their members that the revolution was murdered. The Communists saw their own brothers being shot with the cooperation of the Trade Unions. Strikes in favour of the revolution were prevented, rendered impossible. Do you hold it possible, Comrade, that under such conditions revolutionary workers should remain in these unions? Especially when these latter are utterly inadequate instruments for the revolution! In my opinion this is a physical impossibility. What would you yourself have done, as a member of a political party, that of the Menshevists for instance, if these had acted thus in the revolution? You would have split the Party (if you had not already done so)! You will reply:

This was a political party, it is different in the case of a Trade Union. I believe you are mistaken. In the revolution, during the revolution, every Trade Union, every workers' union even, is a political party – either pro- or counterrevolutionary.

In your article, however, you say, and you will do so now: these emotional impulses must be conquered, for the sake of unity and Communist propaganda. I will show you, by means of concrete examples, that during the revolution this was impossible in Germany. For these questions must also be considered quite concretely. Let us suppose that Germany had 100,000 really revolutionary dock labourers, 100,000 revolutionary metal workers, and 100,000 revolutionary miners; that these were willing to strike, to fight, to die for the revolution, and that the other millions were not. What are these 300,000 to do? They must in the first place unite, and form a fighting league. This you acknowledge. Without organisation workers can do nothing. Now a new league against old unions, even if the workers remain in the old ones, is a split already; if not formally, at any rate actually, in reality. Next, however, the members of the new league need a press, meetings, localities, a salaried staff. This requires heaps of money. And the German workers possess next to nothing. In order to keep the new league going, they must needs, whether they like it or not, leave the old one. Thus we see that, concretely considered, that which you, Comrade, propose, is impossible.

Build on New Foundations.

However, there are better material grounds yet. The German workers who left the Trade Unions, that wished to destroy them, that created the industrial organisations and workers' unions, stood *in the revolution*. It was necessary to fight at *once*. The revolution was there. The Trade Unions refused to fight. What is the good then of saying: remain in the Trade Unions, propagate your ideas, you will grow stronger, and become the majority. Apart from the fact that the minority would be strangled, as is the custom there, this would be quite fine, and also the Left Wing would try it, if there were only time to do so. But it was impossible to wait. The revolution had begun. And it is still going on!

In the revolution (mind, Comrade, it was in the revolution that the German workers split the Party, and created their Workers' Union) the revolutionary workers will always separate themselves from the social-patriots. In the struggle, no other way is possible. No matter what you, and the Moscow Executive, and the International Congress say, and no matter how much you dislike a split in the Party, it will always take place, on psychological and material grounds, because the workers cannot in the long run tolerate the Trade Unions shooting them, and because there has to be fighting.

That is why the Left Wing has created the Workers' Unions; and as they believe that the revolution in Germany is not over yet, but it will proceed to the final victory, they keep them up.

Comrade Lenin, is there another way out, in the workers' movement, when two trends come up, but that of fighting? And when those trends are very divergent, if they oppose one another, is there another way out but secession? Did you ever hear of any other? And is there anything more opposed than revolution and counter-revolution?

For this reason again the KAPD and the General Workers' Unions are quite right.

And, Comrade, have not these secessions, these clearances always been a blessing for the proletariat? Does not this always become evident after a while? I have some experience in this matter. When we as yet belonged to the social-patriotic party we had no influence – after our expulsion we had some – in the beginning, and very soon we won a great, a very great influence. And how about you, the Bolshevists, after the secession? I believe you fared quite well. Small influence at first, very much later on. And all now. It all depends on the economic and political development, whether a group, be it ever so small, does become the most powerful party. If the revolution in Germany lasts, there is a fair hope that the importance and the influence of the workers' unions will surpass all the others. You should not be intimidated by their numbers – 70,000 against seven millions. Smaller groups than these have become the strongest – the Bolshevists, among others!

The industrial unions and workshop organisations, and the Workers' Unions that are based on them and formed from them, why are they such excellent weapons for the revolution in Western Europe, the best weapons even together with the Communist Party? Because the workers act for themselves, infinitely more so than they did in the old Trade Unions, because now they control their leaders, and thereby the entire leadership, and because they have the supervision of the industrial organisation, and thereby of the entire union.

Every trade, every workshop is one whole, where the workers elect their representatives. The industrial organisations have been divided according to economic districts. Representatives have been appointed for the districts. And the districts in turn elect the general board for the entire State.

All the industrial organisations together, no matter to what trade they belong, constitute the one Workers' Union.

This, as we see, is an organisation altogether directed towards the revolution.

If an interval of comparatively peaceful fighting should follow, this organisation might moreover be easily adapted. The industrial organisations would only have to be combined, according to the industries, within the compass of the Workers' Unions.

The Worker has Power.

It is obvious. Here the workers, every worker, has power, for in his workshop he elects his own delegates, and through them he has direct control over the district and State bodies. There is strong centralisation, but not too strong. The individual and the industrial organisation has great power. He can dismiss or replace his delegates at any time, and compel them to replace the higher positions at the shortest notice. This is individualism, but not too much of it. For the central corporations, the districts and government councils have great power. The individual and the central board have just that amount of power, which this present period, in which the revolution breaks out, requires and allows.

Marx writes that under capitalism the citizen is an abstraction, a cipher, as compared to the State. It is the same in the Trade Unions. The bureaucracy, the entire system of the organisation plane ever so far above, and are altogether out of the reach of the worker. He cannot reach them. He is a cipher as compared to them, an abstraction. For them he is not even the man in the workshop. He is not a living, willing, struggling being. If in the old Trade Unions you replace the bureaucracy by other persons, you will see that before long these also have the same character; that they stand high, unattainably high above the masses, and are in no way in touch with them. Ninety-nine out of every hundred will be tyrants, and will stand on the side of the bourgeoisie. It is the very nature of the organisation that makes them so.

Your tactics strive to leave the Trade Unions as they are, "down below," and only to give them other leaders somewhat more of the Left trend, is therefore purely a change "up above." And the Trade Unions remain in the power of leaders. And these, once spoilt, everything is as of old, or at the very best, a slight improvement in the layers up above. No, not even if you yourself, or we ourselves, were the leaders, we would not consent to this. For we wish to enable the masses themselves to become more intelligent, more courageous, self-acting, more elevated in all things. We want the masses themselves to make the revolution. For only thus the revolution can triumph here in Western Europe. And to this end the old Trade Unions must be destroyed.

Industrial Workers Decide.

How utterly different it is in the industrial unions. Here it is the worker himself who decides about tactics, trend, and struggle, and who intervenes if the "leaders" do not act as he wants them to. The factory, the workshop, being at the same time the organisation, he stands continually in the fight himself.

In so far as it is possible under capitalism, he is the maker and the guide of his own fate, and as this is the case with every one of them, *the mass is the maker and leader of its own fight.*

More, infinitely more so, than was ever possible in the old Trade Unions, reformist as well as syndicalist **(1)**.

The industrial unions and workers' unions that make the individuals themselves, and consequently the masses themselves, the direct fighters, those that really wage the war, are for that very reason the best weapons for the revolution, the weapons we need here in Western Europe, if ever we shall be able without help to overthrow the most powerful capitalism of the world.

But, Comrade, these are only the weaker grounds yet, as compared to the last, main actual reason, which hangs closely together with the principles I have indicated at the beginning. And it is this last ground which is decisive for the KAPD and the opposition party in England. These parties strive greatly to raise the spiritual level of the masses and individuals in Germany and England.

They are of the opinion that there is only *one* means to that end. And I should like to know whether you know of another means in the Labour movement? It is the formation of a group! That shows, in the struggle, what the mass should be. That shows, fighting, what the mass *must* be. If you know of another means, Comrade, tell me so. I know none other.

In the Labour movement, and especially, I imagine, in the revolution, there is but one way to prove the example – the example itself, the *deed.*

---

1. It has to be borne in mind, of course, that this new combination of individualism and centralism is not given right away in its completed form, but that it is only springing up now, and is a process, which will be developed only in the struggle itself, and thus perfected.

The comrades of the Left Wing believe that this small group, in its fight against the Trade Unions and against Capitalism, will win the Trade Unions to its side, or, which is also possible, that gradually the Trade Unions will be directed towards a better course.

This can be attained only through the example. For the raising of the German worker to a higher level, therefore, these new organisations are absolutely indispensable.

The new formation, the Workers' Union, must act against the Trade Unions, in exactly the same way as the Communist parties act against the Socialist parties **(2)**.

The servile, reformist, social-patriotic masses can be converted only through example.

Next I come to England: to the English Left Wing.

After Germany, England is nearest to a revolution, not because in that country the situation is revolutionary already, but because the proletariat there is so numerous, and the capitalist and economic conditions most favourable. Only a strong blow is needed there and the fight will begin, a fight which can only end in a victory. And the blow will come. This is felt, this is almost instinctively known by the most advanced workers of England (as we all feel it), and because they feel this, they have founded a new movement, which, whilst manifesting itself in various directions, and searching as yet, just as in Germany – is in general the rank and file movement, the movement of the masses themselves, without, or practically without leaders **(3)**.

Did you observe, Comrade, that this movement has arisen in two of the most advanced countries only? And from the ranks of the workers themselves? And in many places **(4)**. This proves already in itself that it is of natural growth, and not to be stopped!

---

2. With the sarcastic remark that also the Workers' Union cannot be faultless, you make little impression. It is right only in so far that the union must fight for reforms under capitalism. It is not right in so far as the union fights for the revolution.

3. Shop Committees, Shop Stewards, and, especially in Wales, Industrial Unions.

4. That this movement in Germany was made from above is slander.

Struggle in England Essential.

And in England this movement, this struggle against the Trade Unions, is needed more almost than in Germany, for the English Trade Unions are not only a tool in the hands of the leaders, for the maintenance of capitalism, but they are at the same time far more inefficient as a means for the revolution than those of Germany. The way they are conducted dates from the time of the small struggle, often as far back as the 19th or even the 18th century. England not only has industries where 25 Trade Unions exist, but most of the unions fight one another to the death for members!! And the members are utterly without power. Do you also wish to retain these Trade Unions, Comrade Lenin?

Must not these be opposed, split up, and destroyed? If you are against the Workers' Unions you must also be against the Shop Committees, the Shop Stewards, and the Industrial Unions. Whoever is in favour of the latter, is also in favour of the former. For the Communists in either aim at the same things.

The English Communists of the Left Wing wish to use this new trend in the Trade Union movement to destroy the English Trade Unions in their present shape, to alter them, to replace them by new instruments in the class struggle, which can be applied for the revolution. The same reasons that we have brought forward for the German movement holds good here.

In the postscript of the Executive Committee of the Third International to the KAPD, I have read that the EC is in favour of the IWW in America, as long as this latter wishes only political action and affiliation to the Communist Parties. And these IWW need not join the American Trade Unions! But the Executive Committee is against the Workers' Union in Germany; this latter must join the Trade Unions, although it is communist, and works in cooperation with the political party.

And you, Comrade Lenin, are in favour of the rank and file movement in England (although this often causes a split, and although many of its members want the destruction of the Trade Unions!) and against the Workers' Unions in Germany.

Executive Committee's Opportunism.

I can explain your attitude and that of the Executive Committee only by opportunism; and a mistaken opportunism to boot.

It goes without saying that the Left Wing of the Communists in England cannot go as far as in Germany, because in England the revolution has not begun yet. It cannot as yet organise the rank and file movement all over the country into one whole for the revolution. But the English Left Wing is preparing this. And as soon as the revolution comes, the great masses of workers will leave the old Trade Unions as unserviceable for the revolution, and will join the industrial organisations.

And as the Left Communist Wing penetrates everywhere into this movement, seeking to spread the Communist ideas, it raises the workers by means of its example on to a higher level, also there, and already now. And, as in Germany, that is its real aim **(5)**.

The General Workers' Unions, and the rank and file movement, which are both founded on the factories, the workshops, and on these alone, are the forerunners of the Workers' Councils, the Soviets. As the revolution in Western Europe will be very difficult and consequently of probably very long duration, there will be a long period of transition, in which the Trade Unions are no longer any good, and in which there are no Soviets as yet. This period of transition will be filled out with the struggle against the Trade Unions, their re-forming, their replacing by better organisations. You need not fear, we will have ample time!

Once again this will be so, not because we of the Left Wing will it so, but because the revolution must needs have these new organisations. The revolution cannot triumph without them.

Hail the Rank and File Movement.

All hail, therefore, the rank and file movement in England, and the Workers' Unions in Germany, first forerunners of the Soviets

5. You, Comrade, and many with you, use here the argument that the Communists, by leaving the Trade Unions, lose touch with the masses. But is not the closest touch obtained in the workshops? And have not all workshops turned more than ever into debating halls? How can the Left Communists possibly lose touch, then?

in Europe. Good luck to you, the first organisations that, with the Communist parties, will bring the revolution in Western Europe.

You, Comrade Lenin, wish to compel us to use bad weapons here in Western Europe, where we stand alone, without a single ally, against an as yet extremely powerful, extremely organised and armed capitalism, and where we stand in need of the very best of weapons, the very strongest. Where we want to organise the revolution on the shop floor, and on a shop floor basis, you wish to force the miserable Trade Unions on us. The revolution in Western Europe can and must be organised only on the shop floor and on a shop floor basis, because here capitalism has attained such a high economic and political organisation (in all directions) and because the workers (except for the Communist Party) have no other strong weapons. The Russians were armed, and had the poor peasants. What the weapons and the peasants were for the Russians, tactics and the organisation must be for us for the time being. And then *you* recommend the Trade Unions! From psychological, as well as from material grounds, in the midst of the revolution, we *must* fight these Trade Unions, and you try to hinder us in this fight. We can fight only by means of a splitting-up, and you are preventing us. We wish to form groups, that are to be an example, the only way of showing the proletariat what it is we seek, and you forbid this. We wish to raise the proletariat of Europe to a higher level, and you throw stones in our path.

You do not wish them then: the splitting up, the new formations, the higher stage of development! And why not? Because you want to have the big parties, and the big Trade Unions, in the Third International.

To us this looks like opportunism, opportunism of the very worst kind **(6)**.

---

6. Already now the Trade Union question clearly demonstrates where the opportunist tactics of Moscow lead. The members of the Communist Parties are forced to enter the modern Trade Unions (see the thesis accepted on this point). They are forced, therefore, to become scabs and strike-breakers!!! At the same time they must openly support the Syndicalists!!! Instead of openly saying that neither of these organisations are any good, that new ones have to be formed, on the basis of the industries (the theses themselves declare elsewhere that this is what should be done), they adopt this ambiguous attitude. And why? To add masses to the Third International.

Today, in the International, your actions differ widely from what they were in the Maximalist party. This was kept very "pure" (and is so to this day, perhaps). In the International, all elements are to be accepted right away, no matter how poorly communistic they are.

It is the curse of the Labour movement that, as soon as it has acquired a certain "power," it seeks to enlarge this power by unprincipled means. Social-Democracy also was originally "pure" in almost all countries. Most social-patriots of today were real Marxists. By Marxist propaganda the masses were won, and as soon as the party gained "power" they were abandoned.

Just as the Social-Democrats acted at that time, you and the Third International are acting now. Not on a national scale, of course, but internationally. The Russian Revolution has triumphed through "purity," through firmness of principle. Now it has gained power, and through it the international proletariat has obtained power, this power is to be extended over Europe, and immediately the old tactics are abandoned!

Instead of applying the same efficacious tactics in ALL the other countries to the inner strengthening of the Third International, opportunism is again resorted to, as before, in Social-Democracy. All elements are now to be affiliated: the Trade Unions, the Independents, the French Centre, parts of the Labour Party. To preserve the semblance of Marxism, conditions are put that have to be *signed*, and Kautsky, Hilferding, Thomas, etc., are expelled. The great mass, however, the medium quality, is admitted, is driven in by all possible means. And in order that the Centre shall be all the more powerful, the "Left Wing" is not admitted unless it joins that Centre! *The very best revolutionaries*, like the KAPD, are excluded!

And when these huge masses have thus been united on one average line, they proceed to one common advance under an iron discipline, and with leaders that have been tested in this most extraordinary manner. A common advance whither? Into the abyss.

Failure of Second International.

What is the use of the finest principles, of the most splendid Theses of the Third International, if in practice we exercise this opportunism? The Second International also had the finest principles, yet it failed through practice.

We, however, the Left Wing, refuse to do so. In Western Europe we wish first to build very firm, very clear, and very strong (though at the outset perhaps quite small) parties, kernels, just as you did in Russia. And once we have those, we will make them bigger. But we always want them to be very firm, very strong, very "pure." Only thus can we triumph in Western Europe. Therefore we absolutely reject your tactics, Comrade.

You say that we, the members of the Amsterdam Commission, have forgotten or have never known the lessons former revolutions have taught. Well, Comrade, there is one thing about these former revolutions which I remember quite well. It is this: that the extreme "Left" parties have always played a prominent, eminent part in all of them. It was such in the revolution of the Netherlands against Spain, in the English revolution, in that of France, in the Commune, and in the two Russian revolutions.

In accordance with the development of the Labour movement, there are two trends here in the West-European revolution: the radical and the opportunist trend. These can only arrive at sound tactics, at unity, by means of a mutual struggle. The radical trend, however, though in some particulars it may go too far, is much the best. And yet you, Comrade Lenin, go and support the opportunists!

And not only this! The Executive in Moscow, the *Russian* leaders of a revolution that triumphed only through the help of millions of poor peasants, forces these their tactics on the proletariat of Western Europe, which stands and has to stand all alone. And in so doing annihilates the best trend in Western Europe!

What incredible foolishness, and especially what dialectics:

When the revolution in Western Europe breaks out, it will work for you blue wonders! But the proletariat will be the victim.

Counter-revolutionary Trade Unions.

You, Comrade, and the Executive in Moscow, know that the Trade Unions in Western Europe are counter-revolutionary forces. This is evident from your Theses. And yet you wish to retain them. You also know that the Workers' Union, the rank and file movement, are revolutionary organisations. You say yourself, in your Theses, that the industrial organisations must be and are our aim. And yet you want to smother them. You want to destroy the organisations in which the workers, every worker, and therefore the mass, can attain power and strength, and to keep those in which the mass is a dead tool in the hands of the leaders. Thus you strive to bring the Trade Unions in your power, in the power of the Third International.

Why is it you wish to do so? Why do you follow these bad tactics? Because you want masses around you, no matter of what quality, as long as they are masses. Because you believe that if only you have masses obeying you on account of a strict discipline and centralisation, no matter whether they are communist, half communist, or not communist at all, you, the leaders, will win, in a word, because your tactics are leader-tactics.

By criticizing leader-tactics I do not mean to advocate politics without leaders and centralisation, for without these one attains nothing (they are as indispensable as the party). I am criticizing those politics that collect masses, without inquiring into their convictions, their heart; politics that assume that the leaders, once they have great masses around them, will be able to win.

Russian Tactics Useless in Western Europe.

But these politics, which you and the Executive are now following, will lead nowhere in Western Europe. Capitalism here is far too powerful as yet, and the proletariat is much too isolated. These politics will fail here, just as those of the Second International did.

Here the workers themselves must become strong, and, through them, their leaders. Here the evil the leadership-policy, must be seized by the root.

Through these your tactics on the Trade Union question you and the Moscow Executive have proved, to my mind, that *unless you alter these tactics, you cannot conduct the revolution in Western Europe.*

You say that the Left Wing, in following its tactics, can only talk. Well, Comrade, in the other countries the Left Wing has had next to no opportunities as yet to act. But look at Germany, and the tactics and actions of the KAPD in the "Kapp putsch" and with regard to the Russian revolution, and you will have to take those words back.

III. Parliamentarianism

Next we have to take up the defence of the Left Wing on the question of Parliamentarism (1). The same universal theoretical grounds that we dealt with for the Trade Unions, determine the attitude of the Left Wing in this question also. The fact that the proletariat stands alone, the gigantic force of the enemy, and consequently the necessity for the mass to raise itself to a much higher level, and to rely entirely on its own support. I need not repeat these grounds here. Here, however, there are a few more grounds than on the Trade Union question.

Subjects of Bourgeois Democracy.

In the first place, the workers of Western Europe and the working masses in general are completely subjected, as far as ideas are concerned, to the bourgeois system of representation, to parliamentarism, to bourgeois democracy. Much more so than the workers of Eastern Europe. Here bourgeois ideology has taken a strong hold on the whole of social and political life. It has penetrated far more into the heads and hearts of the workers. Here they have already been brought up in that ideology for hundreds of years. These ideas have altogether saturated the workers.

These relations have been very well depicted by Comrade Pannekoek in the Viennese periodical, *Kommunismus*:

> "The experience of Germany places us face to face with the great problem of the revolution in Western Europe. In these countries the old bourgeois method of production, and the corresponding highly developed culture of many centuries, have made a thorough impression on the thoughts and feelings of the masses. Consequently the spiritual and mental character of the masses here is quite different from that of the Eastern countries, where they had not experienced this domination of bourgeois culture. And herein above all lies the difference in the progress of the revolution in the

---

1. Originally I considered this a minor point. The attitude of the Spartakus League, however, at the time of the Kapp putsch, and your opportunist brochure, opportunist even on this question, have convinced me that it is of great importance.

East and in the West. In England, France, Holland, Scandinavia, Italy and Germany, ever since the middle ages there has been a strong bourgeoisie, with petty-bourgeois and primitive capitalist production; whilst feudalism was being defeated, an equally strong, independent peasantry sprang up in the country, which was master in its own small sphere."

On this soil bourgeois civic spiritual life developed into a firm national culture, especially in the coastlands of England and France, which were most advanced by capitalist development. In the nineteenth century capitalism, by bringing the whole of agriculture under its power, and pulling even the most isolated farms into the circle of the world economy, has raised this national culture to a higher level, has refined it, and by means of its spiritual methods of propaganda, the Press, the school, and the Church, has beaten it firmly into the brains of the masses it has proletarianised, both those who were sucked into the cities, and those who were left on the land. This applies not only to the original capitalist countries, but also, though in a somewhat modified form, to America and Australia, where the Europeans founded new States, and to the countries of Central Europe, that had until then stagnated: Germany, Austria, Italy, where new capitalist development could link up with old, obsolete, petty- bourgeois economy, agriculture and culture. In the Eastern countries of Europe capitalism found quite different material and other traditions. Here in Russia, Poland, Hungary, and the region to the east of the Elbe, there was no small, strong bourgeois class dominating spiritual life since time immemorial; primitive agrarian relations with large scale landed property, patriarchal feudalism and village communism determined spiritual life.

Here, on the ideological problem, Comrade Pannekoek has hit the nail on the head. Far better than it has ever been done from your side, he has demonstrated the difference between the east and the west of Europe, from the ideological angle, and has given the cue towards finding revolutionary tactics for Western Europe.

This only need be combined with the *material* causes of the power of our opponents, that is to say with banking capital, and the tactics become perfectly clear.

Workers Win Rights for Possessing Class.

However, there is yet more to be said on the ideological question: civil liberties, the power of parliament, has been won in Western Europe by means of wars for liberty, waged by former generations, by the ancestors. And though at the time these rights were only for citizens, for the possessing class, they were won by the people all the same. The thought of these struggles is to this day a deeply-rooted tradition in the blood of this people. Revolutions are always the deepest memories of a people. Unconsciously the thought that it meant a victory to achieve representation in parliament has a tremendous, silent force. This is especially the case in the oldest bourgeois countries, where long or repeated wars have been waged for freedom: in England, Holland and France. Also, though on a smaller scale, in Germany, Belgium, and the Scandinavian countries. An inhabitant of the East cannot realise, perhaps, how strong this influence can be.

Moreover the workers themselves have fought here, often for years, for universal suffrage, and have thus obtained it, directly or indirectly. This was also a victory, which bore fruit at the time. The thought and the feeling generally prevails, that it is progress, and a victory, to be represented, and to entrust one's representative with the care of one's affairs in Parliament. The influence of this ideology is enormous.

And finally, reformism has brought the working class of Western Europe altogether under the power of the parliamentary representatives, who have led it into war, and into alliances with capitalism. The influence of reformism is also colossal.

All these causes have made the worker the slave of Parliament, to which he leaves all action. He himself does not act any longer **(2)**.

Then comes the revolution. Now he has to act for himself. Now the worker, alone with his class, must fight the gigantic enemy, must wage the most terrible fight that ever was.   No tactics of the

---

2. This great influence, this entire ideology of the West of Europe, of the United States and the British colonies, is not understood in Eastern Europe, in Turkey, the Balkans, etc. (to say nothing of Asia, etc.).

---

leaders can help him. Desperately the classes, all classes, oppose the workers, and not one class sides with them. On the contrary, if he should trust his leaders, or other classes in parliament, he runs a great risk of falling back into his old weakness of letting the leaders act for him, of trusting parliament, of persevering in the old notion that others can make the revolution for him, of pursuing illusions, of remaining in the old bourgeois ideology.

This relationship of the masses to the leaders has also been excellently characterised by Comrade Pannekoek:

"Parliamentarism is the typical form of the kind of fight carried out by means of leaders, in which the masses themselves play but a minor part. Its practice consists in this: that representatives, individual persons, carry on the actual fighting. With the masses it must therefore awaken the illusion that others can do the fighting for them. Formerly the belief was that the leaders could obtain important reforms for the workers through parliament; many had even had the illusion that the members of parliament, by means of laws and regulations, could carry out the transition to Socialism. Today, since parliamentarism acts in a more honest way, the argument is heard that the representatives may do great things in parliament for communist propaganda. Ever again the importance of the leaders is emphasised, and it is only natural that professionals should decide about politics, be it in the democratic guise of congress discussions and resolutions. The history of Social Democracy is a series of fruitless attempts to let the members determine their own politics. Wherever the proletariat goes in for parliamentary action, all this is inevitable, as long as the masses have not yet created organs for self-activity; as long, therefore, as the revolution has not broken out. As soon as the masses can act for themselves, and can consequently decide, the disadvantages of parliamentarism become paramount."

The problem of tactics is how to eradicate the traditional bourgeois way of thinking that saps the strength of the mass of the proletariat; everything which reinforces the traditional view is wrong. The most firmly rooted, most tenacious part of this mental attitude is dependence on leaders, to whom it leaves the decisions in all general questions, and the control of all class matters. Inevitably, parliamentarism has a tendency to crush in the masses the activity necessary for the revolution. No matter what fine speeches are delivered to inspire the workers to revolutionary deeds, revolutionary action does not spring from such words, but from the keen and hard necessity that leaves no other choice whatsoever.

Demands of the Revolution.

The revolution also demands something more than the fighting action of the masses that overthrows the government, and which, as we know, is not under the control of leaders, but can only come from the deeply felt impulse of the masses. The revolution demands that the great questions of social construction be taken in hand, that difficult decisions shall be made, that the entire proletariat be roused to one creative impulse; and this is only possible if first the advance guard, and then an ever greater mass takes things in hand – a mass that is conscious of its responsibilities, that searches, propagates, fights, strives, reflects, considers, dares, and carries out. All this is, however, hard work: so as long as the proletariat thinks there is an easier way, letting others act for it by carrying out agitation from a high platform, by taking decisions, by giving signals for action, by making laws, it will hesitate, and the old ways of thinking and the old weaknesses will keep them pacified.

The workers of Western Europe, let it be repeated a thousand and, if need be, a hundred thousand or a million times – and whoever has not learned and seen it since November 1918 is blind – the West European workers must in the first place act for themselves – in the Trade Unions and also politically, and they must let their leaders act, because the workers stand alone, and because no clever tactics of leaders can help them. The greatest impetus must come from them. Here, for the first time, to a far greater degree than in Russia, *the liberation of the workers must be the work of the workers themselves.* That is why comrades of the Left Wing are right in saying to the German Comrades: don't participate in the elections, and boycott parliament – politically you must do everything for yourselves – you cannot win unless you do so for two, five, or ten years; unless you train yourself to it man by man, group after group, from town to town, from province to province, and finally in the entire land, as a party, a union; as industrial councils, as a mass, and as a class. You cannot win unless finally, through incessant training and fighting, and through defeat, you advance to that stage, the great majority among you, where you can do all this, and where, at last, after all this schooling, you constitute one united mass.

And that is why the comrades of the KAPD were right, perfectly right – history demanded it of them – at once to proceed to a secession, to split the Trade Unions; as this covers the entire political question, there is an urgent need for the fight, the example, the lead.

An Example Needed.

But these comrades of the Left Wing, the KAPD, would have committed a grave mistake had they done nothing but preach and propagate this. Here even more perhaps, than in the case of the party, when the Spartakus League, or rather the Spartakus Zentrale, refused to stand this propaganda of theirs. For what the German slaves, what all workers of Western Europe needed in the first place, was an example. In this nation of political slaves, and in this subjected West European world, there had to be a group that gave the example of free fighters without leaders, that is to say, without leaders of the old type – without members of parliament.

And once again all this must be, not because it is so beautiful, or good, or heroic, but because the German and West-European proletariat stands alone in this terrible fight, without help from any other class, because the cleverness of the leaders is of no avail any longer, because there is but one thing that is needed, the will and firmness of the mass, man for man, woman for woman, and of the mass as a whole.

For this higher motive, and because the opposite tactics, parliamentary action, can but harm this higher cause, infinitely higher than the petty profit of parliamentary propaganda, for this higher motive the Left Wing rejects parliamentarism.

You say that Comrade Liebknecht, if he yet lived, might work wonders in the Reichstag. We deny it. Politically he could not manoeuvre there, because all the bourgeois parties oppose us in one united front. And he could win the workers no better in parliament than outside it. On the other hand, the masses, to a very great extent, would leave everything to be done through his speeches, so that his parliamentary action would have a harmful effect **(3)**.

Big Numbers of no Avail.

It is true that this work of the Left Wing would take years, and those people who for some reason or other, strive for immediate results, big numbers, large amounts of members and votes, big parties, and a powerful (seemingly powerful!) International, will have a rather long time to wait. Those, however, who realise that the victory of the German and West-European revolution can only come, if a very great number, if the mass of the workers believe in themselves, will be satisfied with these tactics.

For Germany and Western Europe they are the only tactics possible. This is particularly true for England.

Comrade, do you know the bourgeois individualism of England, its bourgeois liberty, its parliamentary democracy, as they have grown during some six or seven centuries? Do you really know them? Do you know how utterly they differ from conditions in your country? Do you know how deeply these ideas are rooted in everyone, also in the proletarian individuals of England and its colonies? Do you know into what an immense whole it has developed? Do you know how generally spread it is? In social and personal life? I do not think there is one Russian, one inhabitant of Eastern Europe, who knows them. If you knew them, you would rejoice at those among the English workers who totally break with this greatest political formation of world capitalism.

If this is done with full consciousness, it demands a revolutionary mind, quite as great as that which once broke with Czarism. This rupture with the entire English democracy constitutes the era of the English revolution.

---

3. The example of Comrade Liebknecht is in itself a proof that our tactics are right. *Before* the revolution, when imperialism was as yet at the summit of power, and suppressed every movement by martial law, he could exercise an enormous influence through his protests in parliament; *during* the revolution this was so no longer. As soon, therefore, as the workers have taken their lot into their own hands, we must let go of parliamentarism.

And this is done, as it must inevitably be done in England, with its tremendous history, tradition, and strength; it is done with the utmost firmness of purpose. Because the English proletariat has the greatest power (potentially it is the most powerful on the earth), it makes a sudden stand against the mightiest bourgeoisie of the earth, and with one stroke rejects the whole of English democracy, although the revolution has not yet broken out there.

That is what their vanguard did, just like the German one, the KAPD. And why did they do it? Because they know that they also stand alone, and that no class in all England will help them, and that above all the proletariat itself, and not the leaders, must fight and win there **(4)**.

A Great Day.

It was an historic day, Comrade, when on this June day in London the first Communist Party was founded, and this Party rejected the entire structure and government apparatus of seven hundred years. I wish Marx and Engels could have been present there. I believe they would have felt a great, a supreme joy at seeing how these English workers rejected the English State, the example for all States of the earth, and which for centuries has been the centre and stronghold of world capitalism and rules over one third of humanity; how they reject it and its parliament, though only theoretically as yet.

These tactics are all the more necessary in England because English capitalism supports the capitalism of all other countries, and

---

4. It is true that England has no poor peasants to support capital. But the middle class is correspondingly greater, and is united with capitalism. By means of this advance guard the English proletariat shows how it wants to fight: alone, and against all classes of England and its colonies. And exactly like Germany again: by setting an example. By founding a Communist Party that rejects parliamentarism, and that calls out to the entire class in England: let go of parliament, the symbol of capitalist power. Form your own party and your own industrial organisations. Rely on your own strength exclusively.

This had to be so in England, Comrade; it had to come in the long run. This pride and courage, born out of the greatest capitalism. Now that it comes at last, it comes in full force at once.

will decidedly not scruple to summon auxiliaries from all over the world, against every foreign, as well as against its own proletariat. The fight of the English proletariat, therefore, is a struggle against world capitalism. All the more reason for the English Communists to give the most elevated and brilliant example. To wage an exemplary fight on behalf of the world proletariat, and to strengthen it by example (5).

Thus there has to be everywhere one group that draws all the consequences; such groups are the salt of humanity. Here, however, after this theoretical defence of anti-parliamentarism, I have to answer in detail your defence of parliamentarism. You defend it (from page 36 to 68), for England and Germany. The argumentation, however, holds good only for Russia (and at the very utmost for a few other East-European countries), not for Western Europe. That, as I have said before, is where your mistake lies. That turns you from a Marxist into an opportunist leader. That causes you, the Marxist, radical leader for Russia, and probably a few more East-European countries, to sink

---

5. In England, more even than anywhere else, there is always a great danger of opportunism. Thus also our Comrade Sylvia Pankhurst, who from temperament, instinct and experience, not so much perhaps from deep study, but by mere chance, was such an excellent champion of Left Wing Communism, seems to have changed her views. She gives up anti-parliamentarism, and consequently the cornerstone of her fight against opportunism, for the sake of the immediate advantage of unity! By so doing she follows the road thousands of English Labour leaders have taken before her: the road towards submission to opportunism and all it leads to, and finally to the bourgeoisie. This is not to be wondered at. But that you, Comrade Lenin, should have induced her to do so, should have persuaded her, the only fearless leader of consequence in England, this is a blow for the Russian, for the world revolution.

One might ask why I defend anti-parliamentarism for England, whereas above I have recommended it only for those countries where the revolution has broken out. The answer must be that in the struggle it may often prove necessary to go one step so much to the Left. If, in a country so diseased with opportunism as England, the danger should arise of a young Communist Party falling back into the course of opportunism, through parliamentarism, it is a tactical necessity to defend anti-parliamentarism. And thus in many countries of Western Europe it may continue to be!

---

back into opportunism where Western Europe is concerned. And, if accepted here, your tactics would lead the entire West to perdition. This I will next prove in detail, in answer to your argumentation.

Comrade, on reading your argumentation from page 36 to 68, a recollection constantly occurred to me.

Amongst the Social Patriots.

I saw myself once more at a congress of the old Social-Patriotic Party of Holland, listening to a speech of Troelstra's – a speech in which he depicted to the workers the great advantages of the reformist policy, in which he spoke of the workers that were not social-democratic yet, and that were to be won by compromise; in which he spoke of the alliances that were to be made (only provisionally, of course!) with the parties of these workers, and of the "rifts" in and between the bourgeois parties, of which we were to make use. In just the same way, in almost, nay in absolutely the same words, you, Comrade Lenin, speak for us West Europeans!

And I remember how we sat there, far back in the hall; we the Marxist Comrades, very few in number – only four or five. Henriette Roland Holst, Pannekoek, and a few others. Troelstra spoke persuasively and convincingly, just as you do, Comrade. And I remember how, in the midst of the thundering applause, of the brilliant reformist expositions and the reviling of Marxism, the workers in the hall looked round at the "idiots" and "asses" and "childish fools," names that Troelstra called us at that time – almost the same as you call us now. To all probability things have been practically the same at the Congress of the International in Moscow, when you spoke against the "Left" Marxists. And his words – just like yours, Comrade – were so convincing, so logical, within the compass of his method, that at times I myself thought, yes, he is right.

Usually I was the one to speak for the opposition (in the years up to 1909, when we were expelled). Shall I tell you what I did, when I began to doubt about myself? I had a means that never failed: it was a sentence from the Party Programme:

"You shall ever act or speak in such a way that the class consciousness of the workers shall be roused and strengthened."

And I asked myself: is the class consciousness of the workers roused or not by what the man over there is saying? And then I always knew that at once this was not the case, and that therefore I was right.

It was just the same reading your brochure. I hear your opportunist arguments for cooperation with non-Communist parties, with bourgeois elements, for compromise. And I am carried away. It all seems so brilliant, clear and fine. And so logical as well. But then I consider, as I used to long ago, just one phrase which some time ago I made for myself, for the campaign against the Communist opportunists. It is as follows:

Is what yonder Comrade says the sort of thing that strengthens the will of the masses for action, for the revolution, for the real revolution in Western Europe – yes or no?

And with regard to your brochure, my head and heart answer at the same time: no. Then I know at once, as surely as one can possibly know anything, that you are wrong.

I can recommend this method to the comrades of the Left Wing. Whenever you want to know, Comrades, in the severe struggles ahead of us, against the opportunists of all countries (here in Holland they have been waging for the last three years) whether and why you are right, ask yourself this question!

Lenin's Three Arguments.

In your opposition to us, Comrade, you use only three arguments, that constantly recur all through your brochure, either separately or combined.

They are the following:

1. The advantages of parliamentary propaganda for winning the workers and the petit bourgeois elements to our side.

2. The advantages of parliamentary action for making use of the "rifts" between the parties, and for compromises with some of them.

3. The example of Russia, where this propaganda and the compromise worked so wonderfully well.

Further arguments you have none; I will answer them in turn.

To begin with the first argument, propaganda in parliament. This argument is only of very slight importance, for the non-communist workers, that is to say the social-democrats, the Christian and other bourgeois elements do not, as a rule, read one word in their papers about our parliamentary speeches

Often these speeches are utterly mutilated. With those, therefore, we achieve nothing We only get at the workers through our meetings, brochures and newspapers

Action Speaks Louder than Words.

We, however (I often speak in the name of the KAPD), get at them especially through action (in the time of the revolution of which we speak). In all bigger towns and villages they see us act. They see our strikes, our street fights, our councils. They hear our watchwords. They see our lead. This is the best propaganda, the most convincing. This action, however, is not in parliament!

The non-communist workers, therefore, the small peasants and bourgeois, can be reached quite well also without parliamentary action.

Here one part in particular from your brochure *Infantile Disorder*, must be refuted; it shows where opportunism is already leading you, Comrade.

On page 52 you say that the fact of the German workers coming in masses to join the ranks of the Independent Party, and not the Communist Party, is attributable to the parliamentary action of the Independents. The mass of the Berlin workers, therefore, had been as good as converted through the death of our Comrades Liebknecht and Rosa Luxemburg, through the purposeful strikes and the street fights of the Communists. Only a speech of Comrade Levi in parliament was lacking as yet! Had he but delivered this speech, they would have come to us, instead of to the double-minded Independents! No, comrade, this is not true. They have gone to the double-minds first because they were afraid as yet of the single-minded: the revolution. Because the transition from slavery to freedom lies through hesitation.

Look out, Comrade, you see whither opportunism is already leading you.

Your first argument is of no importance.

And if we consider that parliamentary action (in the revolution, in Germany and England, and all Western Europe) reinforces the workers' idea that their leaders will do things for them, and dissuades them from the idea that they must do everything for themselves, we see that this argument does not only bring no good at all, but that it is exceedingly harmful.

The second argument: the advantage of parliamentary action (in revolutionary periods) for taking advantage of the rifts between the parties, and for compromises with some of them.

An Uncongenial Task.

To refute this argument (especially for England and Germany, but also for all Western Europe), I shall have to go somewhat more into detail than with .the first. It is most uncongenial to me, Comrade, that I should have to do this against you. This entire question of revolutionary opportunism, for it is no longer reformist, but revolutionary opportunism, is a vital question, literally a matter of life and death for us West-Europeans. The matter itself, the refutation, is easy. We have refuted this argument a hundred times, when Troelstra, Henderson, Bernstein, Legien, Renaudel, Van der Velde, etc., all the Social-Patriots, used it. Why Kautsky, when he was still Kautsky, has refuted it. It was the greatest argument of the reformists. We did not think we would ever have to do it against you. Now we have to.

Well then: The advantage of profiting in parliament from the "rifts" is utterly insignificant, for the very reason that for several years, for a score of years, these "rifts" have been insignificant. Those between the big bourgeois and the petty-bourgeois parties. In Western Europe, in Germany and England. This does not date from the revolution. It was so long before, in the period of peaceful evolution. All parties, including the petty-bourgeoisie and the small peasants, had been *against* the workers for a long time already, and between themselves the difference in matters concerning the workers (and consequently on nearly all points), had become very slight, or had often quite disappeared.

This is an established fact, theoretically as well as practically, in Western Europe, in Germany and England.

Theoretically, because capital concentrates in banks, trusts, and monopolies to an enormous degree.

In Western Europe, and especially in England and Germany, these banks, trusts and cartels have assimilated nearly all capital in the industries, commerce, transport, and to a great extent even in agriculture. The whole of industry, including small scale industry, the whole of transport, including the small enterprises, the whole of commerce, big as well as small, and the greater part of agriculture, big and small, has consequently become absolutely dependent on big capital. They have fused with it.

Comrade Lenin says that small commerce, transport, industry and agriculture, waver between capital and workers. This is wrong. It was so in Russia, and it used to be so here. In Western Europe, in Germany and England, they are now so largely, so utterly dependent on big capital, that they no longer waver. The small shop owner, the small industrialist, the small trader, are absolutely in the power of the trusts, the monopolies, the banks. It is from these that they get their goods and credit. And even the small peasant, through his cooperative and his mortgages, is dependent on the trust, the monopoly, and the banks.

Comrade, this part of my argumentation, the argumentation of the "Left Wing," is the most important of all. The entire tactics for Europe and America depend on it.

What elements do they consist of, Comrade, these lower layers that stand nearest to the proletariat? Of shop owners, artisans, lower officials and employees, and poor peasants.

Let us consider what these are in Western Europe! Follow me, Comrade. Not only in a big shop – there the dependence on capital is a matter of course – but in a small one in a poor, proletarian quarter. Look around you. What do you see? Everything: nearly all the goods, clothes, foodstuffs, implements, fuel etc., are products not only of big industry, but often of the trusts. And not only in the cities, but in the country likewise. The small shopkeepers are for the most part storekeepers of big capital. That is to say of banking capital, for this rules the large factories and the trusts.

Look about you in the workshop of a small artisan, no matter whether in the city or the country. His raw materials, the metals, the leather, the wood, etc., come to him from big capital, often even from the monopolies, that is to say from the banks as well. And in so far as the purveyors are small capitalists as yet, these in their turn depend on banking capital.

And the lower officials and employees? The great majority of them in Western Europe is in the employment of big capital, the State, of the municipality, finally therefore also of the banks. The percentage of employees and officials nearest to the proletariat that are directly or indirectly dependent on big capital is very great in Western Europe. In Germany and England, as well as in the United States and the British colonies, it is enormous.

And the interests of these layers are one therefore with those of big capital, that is to say the banks.

I have already dealt with the poor peasants, and we have seen, that for the time being they cannot be won for Communism, for the reasons already mentioned, and also because they are dependent on big capital for their implements, goods, and mortgages.

What does this prove, Comrade?

That modern West-European (and American) society and State have become *one* big, thoroughly organised whole, which is entirely controlled, moved and regulated by banking capital. That society here is a regulated body, capitalistically regulated, but regulated all the same. That banking capital is the blood, flowing through the entire body, and nourishing all its branches. That this body is one, and that capital renders this body enormously strong, and that therefore all the members will stand by it to the very end – all except the proletariat, which makes this blood: surplus value.

Through this dependence of all classes on banking capital and through the enormous strength of banking capital, all the classes are hostile to the revolution, so that the proletariat stands alone.

And as banking capital is the most pliable and elastic force in the world, and increases its power a thousand times through its credit, it upholds and maintains capitalism and the capitalist State, even after this terrible war, after the loss of thousands of billions, and in the midst of conditions that seem like bankruptcy to us.

And it is through this that, with all the more force, it collects all classes around it, combining them into one whole, against the proletariat. And the force and pliability, and the unison of all classes are so great, that they will last long after the revolution has broken out.

Cause of Revolution's Delay.

It is true that capital has been terribly weakened. The crisis is coming, and with it the revolution. And I believe that the revolution will win. But there are two things that still keep capitalism very strong: the spiritual slavery of the masses, and banking capital.

Our tactics, therefore, have to be based on the power of these two things.

And there is one other cause through which organised banking capital rallies all the classes against the revolution. It is the great number of proletarians. All the classes feel that if only they could induce the workers (in Germany alone almost twenty million) to work 10, 12, or 14 hours a day, then there would be a way out of the crisis. That is why they hold together.

These are the economic conditions in Western Europe.

In Russia banking capital did not have this power yet, so there the bourgeoisie and the lower classes did not unite. Consequently, there were real rifts between them. And there the proletariat did not stand alone.

These economic causes determine politics. It is through this that those classes in Western Europe (dependent slaves that they are) vote for their masters, for these big capitalist parties, and that they belong to them. In Germany and England, in Western Europe, these elements have hardly any parties of their own.

All this was very strong already before the revolution and before the war. Now through the war it has become intensified to an enormous extent – through nationalism and chauvinism, but especially through the massive trustification of all economic forces. Through the revolution, however, this tendency – unity of all bourgeois parties with all petty-bourgeois elements and all poor peasants – has again been immensely strengthened.

The Russian Revolution has not been in vain! Now we know everywhere what to expect.

Thus in Western Europe, and especially in England and Germany, the big bourgeoisie and the big peasants, the middle classes and middle peasants, the lower bourgeoisie and the small peasants, are all united against the workers, through monopoly, the banks, the trusts; through imperialism, the war and revolution (6). And, as the labour question encompasses all things, they are united on all questions.

Here, Comrade, I must make the same remark I have already made (in the first chapter) with regard to the peasant question. I know quite well that the little minds in our Party, that lack the strength to base tactics on great, general lines, and consequently base them on the small, particular ones, that these little minds will call the attention to those elements among these layers, that have not yet come under the banner of big capital.

I do not deny that there are such elements, but I maintain that the general truth, the general tendency in Western Europe, is that they are under the banner of big capital. And it is on this general truth that our tactics must be based!

Neither do I deny that there may be "rifts" yet. I only say that the general tendency is, and will be, for a long time after the revolution: unity of these classes. And I say that for the workers in Western Europe it is better to have their attention directed to that unity than to these rifts. For it is they themselves that must in the first place make the revolution, and not their leaders, their Members of Parliament.

Nor do I say that (which the little minds will make of my words) that the real interests of these classes are the same as those of big capital. I know that these classes are oppressed by it.

What I say is simply this:

These classes cling to big capital even more firmly than before, because now they also see the danger of the proletarian revolution ahead.

---

6. It is true that through the war an infinitely greater number of various elements has come down to the ranks of the proletariat. All elements, though as good as any element that is not proletarian, cling desperately to capitalism, and if need be will defend it by armed force, being hostile to Communism.

In Western Europe the domination of capital means to them a more or less sure existence, the possibility of, or at least the belief in, a betterment of their position. Now they are threatened by chaos and the revolution, which for some time to come means worse chaos. That is why they side with capital in the effort to sweep chaos away by every possible means, to save production, to drive the workers to work longer hours, and to endure privation patiently. For them the proletarian revolution in Western Europe is the fall and breakdown of all order, of all security of existence, be it ever so insufficient. Therefore they all support big capital, and will continue to do so for a long time, including during the revolution.

All Classes Fight the Proletariat.

For finally I must yet point out that what I have said applies to the tactics at the beginning and in the course of the revolution. I know that quite at the end of the revolution, when victory draws near and capitalism has been shattered, these classes will come to us. But we must determine our tactics not for the end, but for the beginning and in the course of the revolution.

Theoretically, therefore, all this had to be so.

Theoretically these classes had to cooperate.

Theoretically this is an established fact. But practically as well.

This I will prove next:

For many years already the entire bourgeoisie, all bourgeois parties in Western Europe, also those that belong to the small peasants and middle bourgeoisie, have done nothing for the workers. And they were all of them hostile to the labour movement, and in favour of imperialism, in favour of the war.

For years already there had not been a single party in England, in Germany, in Western Europe, that supported the workers. All were opposed to them; in all matters (7).

---

7. I lack the space here to point this out in detail. I have done it so at length in a brochure entitled *The Basis of Communism*.

There was no new labour legislation. Conditions grew worse instead. Laws were passed against going on strike. Even higher taxes were levied.

Imperialism, colonisation, marinism and militarism were supported by all bourgeois, including the petty-bourgeois parties. The difference between liberal and clerical, conservative and progressive, big and petty bourgeois, disappeared.

Everything which the social-patriots, the reformists said, about the difference between the parties, about the "rifts" between them, was a fraud. And all this has now been brought forward by you, Comrade Lenin! It was a fraud for all countries in Western Europe. This has been best proved in July-August 1914.

At that time they were all one. And the revolution has made them even far more united in practice. Against the revolution, and consequently against all workers, for the revolution alone can bring actual betterment to all workers, against the revolution they all stand together without a single "rift."

And as through the war, the crisis and the revolution, all social and political questions have come to be connected in practice with the question of the revolution, these classes in Western Europe stand together in all questions, and in opposition to the proletariat.

In a word, the trust, the monopoly, the big banks, imperialism, the war, the revolution, have in practice riveted together into one class all the West-European big and petty bourgeois and peasant parties against the workers **(8)**.

Theoretically and practically, therefore, this is an established fact. In the revolution in Western Europe and especially in England and Germany, there are no "rifts" of any considerable importance between these classes.

---

8. We Dutchmen know this only too well. We have seen the "rifts" disappear before our eyes, in our small, but, through our colonies, highly imperialist country. With us there are no longer democratic, Christian, or other parties. Even the Dutch can judge this better than a Russian, who, I regret to say, seems to judge Western Europe after Russia.

Here again I must add something personal. On pages 40 and 41 you criticise the Amsterdam Bureau. You cite a thesis of the bureau. Parenthetically, what you say with regard to this is wrong – all of it. But you also say that the Amsterdam Commission, before condemning parliamentarism, ought to have given an analysis of the class relations and the political parties, to justify this condemnation. Excuse me, Comrade, this was not the task of the Commission. For that on which their thesis is based, to wit that all bourgeois parties in Parliament as well as more outside, had been all along, and were even now, opposed to the workers, and did not show the slightest "rift," all this had been ascertained long ago, and was an established fact for all Marxists. In Western Europe at any rate, there was no need for us to analyse that.

On the contrary, considering you strive for compromise and alliances in Parliament, which would lead us into opportunism, it was your duty to demonstrate that there are any rifts of importance between the bourgeois parties.

You wish to lead us, here in Western Europe, into compromising. What Troelstra, Henderson, Scheidemann, Turati, etc., could not accomplish in the time of evolution, you wish to do during the revolution. It is for you to prove that this can be done.

Opposing Capitalist Forces Unite to Defeat Revolution.

And this not by means of Russian examples; these are easy enough, to be sure, but with West-European examples. This duty you have fulfilled in the most miserable way. No wonder you took almost exclusively your Russian experience, that of a very backward country, not that of the Western Europe of these modern days.

In the entire booklet, in the parts which deal with these very questions of tactics, the Russian examples excepted, to which I will soon proceed, I find but two examples from Western Europe, the Kapp putsch in Germany, and the Lloyd George-Churchill government in England, with the opposition of Asquith.

Very few examples indeed, and of the poorest quality, that there are "rifts" between the bourgeois, and in this case also the social democratic parties!

If ever a proof was needed that between the bourgeois (and in this case also the social democratic parties), there are no important rifts as regards the workers, in the revolution, and here in Western Europe; the Kapp putsch furnishes that proof. The Kappites did not punish, kill and imprison the democrats, the Zentrum people, and the social democrats. And when these came into power again, they did not punish, kill and imprison the Kappites. But both parties killed the Communists!

Communism was too weak as yet. That is why they did not *together* forge a dictatorship. Next time, when Communism will be stronger, they will organise a dictatorship *between them*.

It was and is your duty, Comrade, to point out in what way the Communists could at that time have taken advantage in Parliament of that rift – in such a way, of course, as to benefit the workers. It was and is your duty to tell us what the Communist Members of Parliament ought to have said to make the workers see this rift, and take advantage of it – in such a way, of course, as not to strengthen the bourgeois parties. You cannot do this, because during the revolution there is no rift of any importance. And it is of the time of the revolution that we speak. And it was your duty to point out that if in special cases there should be such rifts, it would be more advantageous to direct the attention of the workers in that direction than to the general tendency towards unity.

And it was and is your duty, Comrade, before beginning to lead us in Western Europe, to show where those rifts are, in England, in Germany, in Western Europe.

This you cannot do either. You speak of a rift between Churchill, Lloyd George, and Asquith, of which the workers are to take advantage. This is altogether pitiful. I will not even discuss this with you. For everyone knows that since in England the industrial proletariat has some power, these rifts have been artificially made by the bourgeois parties and leaders and are yet being made, to mislead the workers, to entice them from the one side to the other, and back again ad infinitum, thus to keep them for ever powerless and dependent. To this end they even at times admit two opponents to the one government, Lloyd George and Churchill. And Comrade Lenin lets himself be caught in this trap, that is well nigh a century old! He strives to induce the British workers to base their politics on this fraud! At the time of the revolution, the Churchills, Lloyd George, and the Asquiths will unite against the revolution, and then you, Comrade, will have betrayed and weakened the English proletariat with an illusion. It was your duty to point out not by means of general, fine and brilliant figures of speech (as in the entire last chapter, on page 72 for instance), but accurately, concretely, by means of clear examples and facts, what those conflicts and differences are – not the Russian ones, nor those that are of no importance, or artificially made, but by means of the actual, important, West-European examples. This you do nowhere in your brochure. And as long as you do not give these, we do not believe you. When you give them we will answer you – until then we say: it is nothing but illusions that mislead the workers, and lead them into false tactics. The truth is, Comrade, that you wrongly assume the West-European and the Russian revolutions to be alike. And for what reason? Because you forget that in the modern, that is to say the West-European and North American States, there is a power that stands above the various kinds of capitalists – the landowners, industrial magnates, and merchants banking capital. This power, which is identical with imperialism, unites all capitalists, including the small peasants and bourgeois.

One thing, however, remains to you. You say there are rifts between Labour parties and the bourgeois parties, and that these can be made use of. That is right.

We might aver, to be sure, that these differences between the social democrats and bourgeois in the war and in the revolution have been very slight and have disappeared in most cases! But they might be there. And they may arise yet. Of those we must therefore speak. Especially as you put it, the "pure" English Labour government, Thomas, Henderson, Clynes, etc., in England, against Sylvia Pankhurst, and the possibly "pure" socialist government of Ebert, Scheidemann, Noske, Hilferding, Crispien, Cohn, against the KAPD (9).

---

9. It is yet the question whether these "pure" Labour governments will come here. Maybe that here again you let yourself be misled by the Russian example – Kerensky. Later in this letter, I will point out why in this case, in the March days in Germany, this "pure" socialist government was not to be supported all the same.

You say that your tactics, which direct the workers' attention towards these Labour governments, encouraged them to promote their formation, are clear and effective; whilst ours, which are opposed to their formation, are harmful.

No, Comrade, our attitude with regard to these cases of "pure" Labour government where the rift between these parties of workers and those of the bourgeoisie became a split, is again quite clear, and profitable, to the revolution.

It is possible that we shall allow such a government to exist. It can be necessary, it can mean progress for the movement. If this is so, we cannot proceed any further yet, we will let it exist, criticising them as keenly as possible, and replace them by a Communist government as soon as we can. But to promote its arrival in Parliament and in elections, this will not do in Western Europe.

And we will not do this, because in Western Europe and in the revolution the workers stand all alone. For that reason everything – do you understand this? – everything HERE depends on their will for action, on their clearness of brain. And because of these, your tactics of compromising with the Scheidemanns and Hendersons, with the Crispiens and their followers among the English Independents, of the opportunist Communists of the Spartacus League or the BSP – because these tactics inside and outside Parliament confuse heads, here in Western Europe and in the revolution – making the workers elect someone whom they know beforehand to be an impostor, and because our tactics on the other hand make them clear-sighted, by showing them the enemy as enemy, because of all this and, even at the risk of losing a representative in Parliament in periods of illegality, or of missing the benefit, of a "rift" (in Parliament!), we in Western Europe, and under the present conditions, choose our tactics and reject yours.

Here again your advice leads to confusion, and awakens illusions.

But what about the members of the social democratic parties, the German Independents, the Labour Party, and the Independent Party? Must not those be won?

These, the working class and petty-bourgeois elements among them, will be won by us, the Left Wing, in Western Europe, through our propaganda, our meetings and our press, and especially through our example, our slogans, our action on the shop floor. In the revolution, those who are not won thus, through our action, through the revolution, are lost anyway, and can go to the devil. These social-democratic, Independent Labour Parties in England and Germany consist of workers and petty-bourgeois elements. The first, the workers, can all be won in the long run. The petty-bourgeois elements only to a very slight extent, and are of little economic importance; these few will be won over by our propaganda, etc. The majority of them – and it is on these that Noske and his conjurers rely above all – belong to capitalism, and, in proportion to the revolution's advance, they rally all the closer around it.

Workshop, not Parliament, the Battle-ground.

But does the fact that we do not support them at the elections imply that we are cut off from the Labour Parties, the independents, the social democrats, the Labour Party, etc.? On the contrary, we seek alliance with them as much as we can. On every occasion we summon them for common action: for the strike, the boycott, for revolt, street fights, and especially for the workers' councils, the industrial councils. We seek them everywhere. Only not in parliament, as we used to do. This, in Western Europe, belongs to a past epoch. But in the workshop, in the union and in the street – that is where we find them. That is where we win them. This is the new practice, succeeding social democratic practice. It is the Communist practice.

You, Comrade, wish to bring the social democrats, the Independents, etc., into Parliament in order to show that they are deceivers. You wish to use Parliament to show that it is of no use.

You seek to slyly deceive the workers. You put the rope round their neck and let them hang. We help them to avoid the rope. We do this because here we are able to do so. You follow the tactics of the peasant races; we those of the industrial races. This is no scorn, and no mockery. I believe that with you it was the right way. Only you should not – either in this small matter, or in the great question of parliamentarism – force on us what was good in Russia but leads to destruction here.

Finally I have only one remark to make: you say, and you have often upheld it, that in Western Europe the revolution can only begin *after* these lower classes adjacent to the proletariat have been sufficiently shaken, neutralised or won over. As I have demonstrated that they cannot be shaken, neutralised or won at the beginning of the revolution, this latter, if your statement was correct, would be impossible. This has been told to me over and over again, from your side, and also by Comrade Zinoviev. Fortunately, however, here also your observation in the most important of questions which determine the revolution, is false. And it again proves that you see all things exclusively from the East-European point of view. I will make this clear in the last chapter.

I herewith believe to have proved that your second argument for parliamentarism is for the most part an opportunistic fraud, and that in this respect parliamentarism must now be replaced by another method of fighting, one that lacks its drawbacks and possesses greater advantages.

I recognise that in this one point your tactics can have some advantages. The Labour Government can produce some good, greater clarity. And in illegal times your tactics can be profitable. We recognise that. But just as once we needed to say to the revolutionists and reformists: we prize the development of self-consciousness in the workers above everything, even above small advantages. We now say to you, Lenin and your "Right" comrades: we prize above all the ripening of the masses towards will and deed. Hereto all things have to be made subservient in Western Europe. We will see who is right, the "Left" or Lenin. I do not doubt one moment. We will defeat you, as we did Troelstra, Henderson, Renaudel and Legien.

This here is the place to discuss the mutual relationship between party, class and mass in Western Europe.

This matter is also of the greatest importance: as important as the power of banking capital, and the *unity* of all great and small bourgeois classes it engenders. The relation between party, class and mass in Western Europe differs widely from that of Russia, and like the unity of the bourgeois classes it is due to the power of banking capital.

Our tactics must be directed toward and based on a true understanding of that relationship. Whoever does not understand this relationship, cannot understand the tactics for Western Europe.

Let us again take Germany as an example. Not only because, with England, it is industrially the most highly developed country, but also because it offers the most developed statistics.

As we have often observed already, it has a proletariat of about twenty million actual workers: about fourteen million industrial and some six million agricultural. What does this mean? That, counting children, non-workers and the aged, this proletariat comprises at least half – and probably more – of the total population of Germany.

We have seen, however, that in the revolution the proletariat stands alone, and that the opponents of the proletariat, of the revolution, by virtue of their arms and their organisation, even to this day are so powerful that they can only be conquered by means of the unity of the entire proletariat. And because of banking capital their power is such that unity alone does not suffice: that a conscious, determined unity, a truly Communist unity is needed.

Two facts therefore are certain: the proletariat is very numerous, it comprises more than half the population; and the opposition, in spite of this, is so powerful that the unity of the proletariat, real Communist unity is necessary.

Only thus can Capitalism be overthrown, and can the revolution conquer.

What follows from these two facts?

Firstly, that the dictatorship of a Party, of a Communist Party, cannot exist here in Germany, as it did in Russia, where a few thousand dominated the proletariat. Here, in order to conquer capital, the dictatorship must be exercised by the class itself, the entire class **(10)**.

It is not, we insistently repeat, for any radical romantic, aesthetic, heroic or intellectual reason, but for the most simple and

---

10. The Russian Communist Party at the time of Yudenitch's and Denikin's attacks, numbered 13,287 men, not one ten thousandth part of the population of 150 million. Through special weeks of propaganda the number, by January 1920, increased to 220,000. Now it is no more than 600,000, 52% of which are workers.

concrete fact—one moreover that is only too much felt by the German proletariat: that highly organised German monopoly banking capital is so powerful, it unites the entire bourgeoisie.

The same cause that unites the entire bourgeoisie makes it necessary that the entire class should exercise its dictatorship.

A United Proletariat Necessary.

From the above mentioned causes there follows secondly: that at the beginning and during the course of the revolution the masses are divide into two hostile camps. By masses we mean the proletariat and the other working class combined.

These latter (petty-bourgeois, peasants, intellectuals, etc.) in the beginning and during the course of the revolution are hostile to the greater part of the proletariat. Between the proletariat on the one side and the rest of the masses on the other, there is an antithesis. Class and mass in Western Europe are not one, nor can they become so at the start, and in the first stages of the revolution.

Finally from the numerical relations of the proletariat towards the other classes, and from the fact that the proletariat must be united in order to win, there follows, as I have shown above, that the relative importance of the class, as opposed to the power of leaders, must be very great; that the power of the leaders, with regard to that of the class, must be small, and likewise that in all likelihood in Germany power cannot come into the hands of some few leaders.

If we consider the character of German industry, its concentration in great numbers of centres, this goes without saying. How great, how numerous the leadership will be, cannot as yet be ascertained, it can only be stated that it will be extended over a great number of persons.

And thus, after Germany, it is in the first place in England – and, though to a lesser degree, all over Western Europe.

And this fact that the entire class must exercise its dictatorship, how does it affect the Communist Party?

From this fact follows that the task of the Communist Party in Western Europe consists almost exclusively of preparing the class and making it conscious for the revolution and the dictatorship.

In all its actions and all its tactics the Party must always bear in mind that the revolution must be made, and the dictatorship exercised not by the Party alone, but by the class.

The task can only be fulfilled if the Communist Party consists of politically truly conscious and convinced revolutionaries, who are ready for any deed, any sacrifice, and if all the half-baked and wavering elements are kept off by means of its programme, by action, and especially by the very tactics.

For only thus, only by preserving this purity, the Party will be able to make the class truly revolutionary and Communist, through its propaganda, its slogans, and by taking the lead in all actions. The Party can take the lead only by being always absolutely pure itself.

How large the Communist Party will become through this action cannot be predetermined. We desire, of course, that it may be as big as possible. But the entire tactics and the entire struggle must be dominated by this principle: better a thousand members that are good, than a hundred thousand that are bad. For these latter cannot accomplish the revolution and the dictatorship of the proletariat.

It all depends on the purity and the firmness of the Communist Party, how far its power will reach; and how much it will influence the masses. Also the quality of the leaders depends to some degree on its tactics.

In other words, Comrade Lenin, we must never follow the tactics you followed in 1902 and 1903, when you formed the Party that has made the revolution.

Menshevist Tactics would Ruin Proletariat.

All the social democrats of Russia at that time were of the opinion that a proletarian organisation ought to be created, and they agreed that this organisation was to be obtained by means of a blind imitation of German social democracy; all this has finally crystallised into the Menshevist Party. The later Menshevists dreamed of building a big Labour Party, in which the masses would be able to find the road to their action. Such a party would have to accept all those who adopted its programme, it would have to be democratically conducted, and would find its revolutionary way by means of free criticism, and free discussion. It was against this alluring image,

Comrade Lenin, that you directed all the blows of your criticism, and not only because such a party was impossible under Czarism, and an illusion, but mainly because "behind this illusion, there lurked the immense danger of opportunism."

The tactics of the Menshevists would mean that the most wavering and hesitating elements would obtain a decisive influence on the party of the proletariat. This you wished to prevent, and that is why you took care that the programme (in the well known first article), and the tactics also, should always be such that this was impossible **(11)**.

As you did then, we of the Left Wing wish to do now in the Third International. Through our very programme and tactics we wish to chase away all vacillating and opportunist elements; we only wish to accept the truly Communist, truly revolutionary ones, we wish to carry out truly communist action. And all this exclusively with a view to inspiring the entire class with communist spirit, and of preparing it for the revolution and the dictatorship.

This latter, the preparation, is of course a process – a process of interaction. Every action, every partial revolution advances the class, brings it nearer to the party, and the stronger class means greater strength for each new struggle, and also for the party. Thus party, a class come into ever closer contact, and finally they grow into one whole.

This, therefore, is our purpose: the Party, small or large, does everything in its power to further the ripening of the class for revolution and dictatorship, as this class stands alone in the revolution, without the help of the peasants.

However, there is yet another means to obtain this. Besides the political party we have as our weapon the Arbeiter-Union, based on the industrial organisation. What the party is for political action, the Union is for economic action.

And just as the numerical and class relations for Germany and Western Europe, which I have quoted, clearly demonstrate that the party cannot exercise the dictatorship, so these figures, these class relations, this unity of all bourgeois classes against the revolution, this

---

11. The quotations are from Radek.

---

inevitable unity of the proletariat against them, and this necessity of the entire class exercising the dictatorship, and becoming for the most part communist, demonstrate the iron necessity that no Trade Union, nor Arbeiter-Union or Industrial League, nor IWU or Shop Stewards' Movement can ever presume to exercise the dictatorship.

They, both of them, party as well as Arbeiter-Union, each in its own sphere, and with every possible mutual support, must do all they can to prepare the class. For the time being, Party and Union are separate as yet. For, like all Trade Unions, the Union also has to fight for small improvements, and is therefore constantly exposed to opportunist and reformist influences. Only a truly communist party can subordinate everything to the revolution.

From the necessity of this development in Western Europe (which has sprung up through the power of banking capital), it is also clearly evident that those who already now in the beginning and course of the revolution wish to place the Arbeiter-Union, the Industrial Union, the industrial organisation, above the Party, or who even wish to abolish the latter, are wrong.

Gradually, as the Party grows stronger, as the Union grows, as the class becomes more and more communist, as the revolution approaches its goal, class, party and Arbeiter-Union or Industrial Union closely approach one another. In the end the Party, the Union and the class are all equivalent, and are blended into one whole.

Finally, of course, the power and the unity of all bourgeois classes, and the necessary unity of the entire proletariat, make strong centralisation and strict discipline, in the Party as well as in the Union, absolutely necessary.

It is the task of the German and English, the West-European and American proletariat to combine centralisation and discipline with the strictest control of, with power over, the leadership.

For only thus can the West-European and American proletariat conquer, through the blending of centralisation in the leadership, and the control of the membership.

It need hardly be explained here that also after the revolution the dictatorship of the entire class, and the communist spirit of the whole proletariat in Western Europe and America are absolutely necessary. For here the counterrevolution is so powerful, that if these two conditions were not fulfilled – if, for instance, a new class of rulers sprung up, out of the intellectuals and the bureaucracy – the revolution would soon perish. Now already the tactics must be on the lookout to prevent this.

How different from Russia all this is!

How different from Russia where, as a result of the economic conditions, as a result of class relations – and rightly, therefore – a handful of people rule the Party, where an infinitesimally small party rules the class, and a minutely small class the entire nation; where no Arbeiter-Union is needed, where the class, and the great majority of the remaining working masses, the small peasants, were one with the revolution!

Whoever fails to understand from the productive and class relations of Western Europe what the relations between the leaders, the party, the class and the masses are, does not understand a thing of the revolution in Western Europe, nor of its necessary stipulations. Whoever wishes to conduct the West European revolution according to the tactics and by the road of the Russian revolution, is not qualified to lead it.

The Left Wing Tactics.

From these West-European, and to some extent also from the American and Anglo-Colonial relations, it is therefore perfectly obvious that there is only one kind of tactics that in Western Europe (and North America) can lead to victory, and these are the tactics of the Left Wing, in the name of which I speak. For these claim that the leaders shall have relatively little power in relation to the class, and the class shall have relatively far greater power. They say that for the time being the class and the rest of the masses cannot be one. They claim that the entire class shall become truly communist, through truly communist propaganda, that therefore party and class shall become one. These, in order to obtain that end, wish to destroy the bourgeois Trade Unions, and replace them by communist industrial organisations, thus making those organisations, substitutes for the Trade Unions, the greatest of class organisations (in Germany they number ten million proletarians already), equal to the class. They are against parliamentarism, thus making every worker, and consequently the entire proletariat, independently revolutionary, which is to say communist.

They, the Left party, act in perfect accordance therefore with class relations as they really are in Western Europe, and are entirely in the right against the Executive Committee, the Congress of the Third International, and you, Comrade Lenin.

Only quite recently you said to a British delegation that in England a quite small Communist Party would be able to accomplish the revolution. Here, again, you speak as a Russian, and judge things by the Russian example. And it is on such mistaken notions that the tactics of the Executive and of the International are based! **(12)**.

Those however who think, and say, and propagate these views, do not understand class relations in Western Europe and North America **(13)**.

12. I point out here the contradiction between this opinion and the effort of winning millions of wavering elements to the Third International. This contradiction is another proof of the opportunism of your tactics.

13. A very strong proof of how the Board of the Third International judges all things from the Russian standpoint, is the following: after the German revolution had been beaten down, after the Bavarian and Hungarian revolutions had been crushed, Moscow said to the German and Hungarian proletariat:

"Be comforted, and bear up, for in March and July 1917, we were also defeated; but in November we won. As it went with us, it will go with you."

And to be sure, this time again Moscow is saying the same to the Czecho-Slovakian workers. But the Russians won in November exclusively because the poor peasants no longer supported Kerensky! Where, Executive Committee, are the millions of poor peasants in Germany, Bavaria, Hungary, and in Czecho-Slovakia? There are none. Your words are just utter nonsense. The perniciousness of these Moscow tactics, however, does not lie solely in that they console the workers by means of a false image, but more especially in the fact that they fail to draw the right conclusion from the defeat in Germany, Bavaria, Hungary and Czecho-Slovakia. The lesson they teach is this:

"Destroy your Trade Unions, and form industrial unions, thus rendering your Party and your class strong internally."

Instead of this lesson, however, we only hear: "It will go with you as it did with us!." Is it not high time that, against these Moscow tactics , there should arise, all over Western Europe, one firmly organised, iron opposition? It is a question of life and death for the world revolution itself. And also for the Russian revolution.

To these observations I need only add that where I speak of the unity of party and class, that is attained at last, and of the possibility of the entire proletariat in Western Europe and America becoming communist, I mean unity as big as possible, and a large part of the proletariat. I represent total unity and the entire proletariat as the Ideal, as the goal towards which we must tend, as the aim of our tactics. In all probability it will be impossible and unnecessary to completely achieve it. But the unity of party and class, and the portion of the proletariat that has to become communist, are so immeasurably greater here than in Russia, that this ideal in the tactics must be brought to the fore **(14)**.

Lenin's Third Argument.

Next I come to your third argument: the Russian examples. You mention them repeatedly (on pp. 6-9 they occur several times). I have read them with the greatest attention, and, as I admired them before, I do now. I have been on your side ever since 1903. Also when I did not know your motives as yet – the connections being cut off – as at the time of the Brest-Litovsk peace, I defended you with your own motives. Your tactics were certainly brilliant for Russia, and it is owing to these tactics that the Russians have triumphed. But what does this prove for Western Europe? Nothing, according to my idea, or very little. The Soviets, the dictatorship of the proletariat, the methods for the revolution and for reconstruction, all this we accept. Also your international tactics have been – so far at least – exemplary. But for your tactics for the countries of Western Europe it is different. And this is only natural.

How could the tactics in the East and West of Europe possibly be the same? Russia, a chiefly agricultural country, but with an industrial capitalism that was only partially highly developed, and very small compared to the land. And, moreover, fed to a large extent by foreign capital! In Western Europe, and especially in England and Germany, it is just the opposite. With you: still all the old-fashioned forms of capital, from usury capital upwards. With us: almost exclusively a highly developed banking capital.

14. With regard to this we must bear in mind that here we are always speaking of a disarmed proletariat. If through some reason or other, through a new war, or later on, in the course of the revolution, the proletariat should once more obtain arms, the above-mentioned conditions do not count.

With you: immense remains of feudal and pre-feudal times, and even from the time of the tribe, of barbarism. With us, and especially in England and Germany: all things, agriculture, commerce, transport, industry, under the domination of the most developed capitalism. With you: immense remains of serfdom, the poor peasants, and in the country a declining middle class. With us: even the poor peasants in connection with modern production, transport, technique and exchange. And in the city as well as in the country the middle class, including the lower layers, in direct contact with the big capitalists.

You still have classes with which the rising proletariat can unite. The very existence of these classes helps. The same applies of course to the political parties. And with us, nothing of all this.

Of course, compromising in all directions, as you so captivatingly describe it, even making use of the rifts between the Liberals and the landowners, was alright for you. With us it is impossible. Consequently the difference in tactics between the East and the West. Our tactics fit our conditions. They are just as good as yours were under Russian conditions.

I find your Russian examples especially on pages 12, 13, 26, 27, 37, 40, 51 and 52. But no matter what these examples may mean for the Russian trade union question (p 27), for Western Europe they mean nothing at all, as here the proletariat needs far stronger weapons. As far as parliamentarism is concerned, your examples have been taken from a period when the revolution had not broken out (pp. 16, 26, 41 and 51 for instance), and these, therefore, either do not apply to the point in question, or, in so far as you could use the parties of the poor peasants and petty-bourgeoisie, they are so different from conditions here (pp. 12, 37, 40, 41 and 51), as to mean nothing to us **(15)**.

It seems to me, Comrade, that your utterly wrong judgment, the utterly mistaken conception of your book, and no less the tactics of the Executive in Moscow, are to be attributed exclusively to the fact that you do not know enough about relations over here, or rather that

---

15. To deal with all these Russian examples would be too monotonous. I request the reader to read them all over. He will see that what I have said above is right.

you fail to draw the right conclusions from what you know, that you judge things too much from the Russian point of view.

This means, however – and it should be emphasised here once again, as the fate of the West-European proletariat, the world proletariat, the world revolution depends on this – that neither you, nor the Moscow Executive are able to direct the West- European and consequently the World Revolution, as long as you adhere to these tactics.

You ask: is it possible that you, who wish to reform the world, cannot even form a fraction in parliament?

Labour Movement in False Grooves.

We answer: this book of yours is a proof in itself that whoever tries to do the latter is bound to lead the Labour movement into false grooves, into ruin.

The book deludes the workers of Western Europe by means of illusions, of the impossible; compromise with the bourgeois parties in the revolution.

It makes them believe in something that does not exist: the possibility of the bourgeois parties being divided in Western Europe, in the revolution. It makes them believe that here a compromise with the social patriots and the wavering elements in parliament can lead to any good, whereas it brings hardly anything but calamity.

Your book leads the West-European proletariat back into the morass, from which at the cost of the greatest efforts it has not yet escaped, but is beginning to escape.

It leads us back into the morass, in which men like Scheidemann, Clynes, Renaudel, Kautsky, MacDonald, Longuet, Vandervelde, Branting and Troelstra have landed us. (It must inevitably fill all these with great joy, and bourgeois parties likewise, if they understand it). This book is to the communist revolutionary proletariat what Bernstein's book has been for the pre-revolutionary proletariat. It is the first book of yours that is no good. For Western Europe, it is the worst book imaginable.

We, comrades of the Left Wing, must stand close together, must start everything from below upward, and must criticise as keenly as possible all those that in the Third International do not go the right way **(16)**.

Thus the conclusion to be drawn from all these arguments about parliamentarism, is as follows: your three arguments for parliamentarism either mean very little, or are wrong. And, as in the Trade Union question, your tactics also on this point are disastrous for the proletariat. And with these mistaken or insignificant motives you hide the fact that you are bringing hundreds of thousands of opportunists into the Third International.

IV. Opportunism in the Third International

The question of opportunism in our own ranks is of such immense weight that I must deal with it more at length.

Comrade! With the establishment of the Third International, opportunism has not died in our ranks either. We see it in all Communist parties in all countries. Also it would be truly miraculous and against all the laws of development if that which killed the Second International did not live in the Third.

On the contrary, just as the fight between anarchism and social democracy was fought in the Second International, that between opportunism and revolutionary Marxism will be fought in the Third.

This time again Communists will go into parliament to become leaders. Trade Unions and Labour parties will be supported for the sake of votes in the elections. Instead of parties being founded for Communism, Communism will be used to found parties. But parliamentary compromises with social patriots and bourgeois elements will once more come into use, as after all the revolution in Western Europe is going to be a slow process. Freedom of speech will be suppressed, and all good Communists expelled. In a word, all the practice of the Second International will come to life again.

---

16. Personally I believe that in countries where the revolution is far off as yet, and the workers are not yet strong enough to make it, parliamentarism can still be used. The sharpest criticism of the parliamentary delegates is necessary in that case. Other comrades, I believe, are of a different opinion.

The Left Wing must oppose this; it has to be there, to wage this fight, as it was there in the Second International. Herein the Left Wing must be supported by all Marxists and revolutionaries, even if they are of the opinion that the Left Wing is mistaken in detail – for opportunism is our greatest enemy. Not only, as you say (p. 13) outside, but also within our ranks.

It would be a thousand times worse, that opportunism, with its devastating effect on the soul and the strength of the proletariat, should again slip in, than that the Left Wing should be too radical. The Left Wing, even though at times it goes too far, always remains revolutionary. The Left Wing will alter its tactics as soon as they are not right. The opportunist Right will grow ever more opportunist, will sink ever further into the morass, will corrupt the workers to an ever greater extent. Not in vain have we learned from twenty-five years of struggle.

Opportunism is the plague of the Labour movement, the death of the revolution. Opportunism has brought about all evils; reformism, the war, the defeat and the death of the revolution in Hungary and Germany. Opportunism is the cause of disaster. And it exists in the Third International.

What do I need so many words for? Look around you, Comrade. Look into yourself, and into the Executive Committee! Look into all countries of Europe.

Feeble Criticism.

Read the papers of the British Socialist Party, now the Communist Party. Read ten, twenty numbers of this paper; read the feeble criticism against the Trade Unions, the Labour Party, the Members of Parliament, and compare this to the paper of the Left Wing. A comparison between these two will show you that opportunism is approaching the Third International, in immense masses. Once more (through support of the counter-revolutionary workers) to obtain power in Parliament. A power after the pattern of the Second International. Remember too that soon the USP will enter the Third International, and numerous other Centre parties besides! Do you not believe that if you compel these parties to expel Kautsky that a swarm of tens of thousands of other opportunists will come? The entire measure of this expulsion is childish. An innumerable stream of opportunists is approaching **(1)** – especially since your brochure.

Look at the Dutch Communist Party, once called the Bolshevists of Europe. And rightly so, taking into account the conditions. Read the brochure about the Dutch Party, how utterly already it has been corrupted by the opportunism of the Second International. During the war, and after it, and even to this day, it has pledged itself to the Entente. This once brilliant party has become an example of equivocality and deceit.

But look at Germany, Comrade, the land where the revolution has started. There opportunism lives and thrives. We were utterly amazed to hear that you defended the attitude of the KPD during the March days. But fortunately we learned from your brochure that you did not know the actual course of development. You sanctioned the attitude of the KPD-Zentrale, that offered loyal opposition to Ebert, Scheidemann, Hilferding and Crispien, but you evidently did not know, at the time of writing the brochure, that this happened at the same moment Ebert organised troops against the German proletariat, whose general strike was still spread all over Germany, and in which the great majority of the Communist mass strove to bring the revolution, if not to victory (perhaps this was hardly possible as yet), at any rate to a higher strength. Whilst the mass by means of strikes and armed revolt, conducted the revolution into a further stage (there has never been anything more hopeful or gigantic than the revolt in the Ruhr region, and the general strike), the leaders offered parliamentary compromises. In so doing they supported Ebert against the revolution in the Ruhr region **(2)**. If ever an example proved how damnable the use of parliamentarism is in the revolution, this is it. You see, Comrade, that is parliamentary opportunism, that is compromise with the social patriots and the Independents, which we refuse to accept, and which you try to further.

1. In Halle, in one day alone, 500,000 new members came under leaders which only a short while before they themselves had recognised to be worse than the Scheidemann lot. And in Tours, three quarters of the French Socialist Party joined, which until quite recently were for the most part social patriots.

2. Comrade Pannekoek, who thoroughly knows Germany, had predicted this. If the leaders of the Spartakus League were placed before the choice between Parliament and Revolution, they would choose Parliament.

And, Comrade, what has already become of the industrial councils in Germany? You and the Executive of the Third International had advised the Communists to unite with all the other trends, in order to obtain the leadership of the Trade Unions. And what has happened? The opposite. The industrial Zentrale has well-nigh developed into an instrument of the Trade Unions. The Trade Unions are an octopus, strangling everything living that comes within its reach.

Comrade, if you read and investigate everything that is being done in Germany, in Western Europe, I have full confidence that you will come over to our side. Just as I believe that your experiences in the Third International will convert you to our tactics.

However, if opportunism proceeds thus in Germany, how will it be in France and England!

You see, Comrade, these are the leaders we do not want. That is the unity of mass and leader that we do not want. And that is the iron discipline, the military obedience, submission and servility that we do not want.

Permit us to add here one word to the Executive Committee, and especially to Radek: the Executive Committee has had the insolence to demand of the KAPD that they should expel Wolffheim and Laufenberg, instead of leaving them to settle this for themselves. It has threatened the KAPD, and has pandered to the central parties, such as the USP. But it did not demand of the Italian Party that it should expel the Zentrale which, through its offer, was partly responsible for the murder of Communists in the Ruhr region. It did not demand of the Dutch Party that it should expel Wijnkoop and Van Ravesteyn, who during the war, offered Dutch ships to the Entente. This does not mean to say that I myself wish those comrades to be expelled. On the contrary, I hold them to be good comrades, who have gone wrong only because the development, the beginning of the West-European revolution, is so terribly difficult. We, all of us over here, still make many big mistakes. Moreover, expulsion at present, from this International, would be of no avail.

I only point this out to demonstrate by another example how fiercely opportunism is raging already in our own ranks. For the Moscow Central Committee has committed this injustice against the KAPD only, because for its opportunist world tactics it did not want the really revolutionary elements, but the opportunist Independents, etc.. It has deliberately used the tactics of Wolffheim and Laufenberg against the KAPD for the most miserably opportunist of reasons, although it knew that the KAPD did NOT agree with those tactics. Because it wants to have masses around it, like the Trade Unions and the political parties, no matter whether those masses are communist or not.

Two other actions of the Third International prove clearly where it is drifting. The first is the expulsion of the Amsterdam Bureau, the ONLY group of revolutionary Marxists and theoreticians in Western Europe, that has never wavered. The second section, which is almost more serious, is the treatment of the KAPD, the ONLY party in Western Europe which, as an organisation, as a whole, from its very origin onwards, has conducted the revolution as it should be conducted. Whilst the Centre parties, the Independents, the French and English Centre, who always betrayed the revolution, were allured by all possible means, the KAPD, the real revolutionaries, were treated as enemies. These are bad signs, Comrade.

In a word: the Second International is still alive, or alive again, in our midst. And opportunism leads to ruin. And because this is so, and because opportunism is very strong amongst us, far stronger than I could ever have imagined, the Left Wing has to be there. Even if there should be no other good reasons for its existence, it would have to be there as an opposition, to counterbalance opportunism.

Alas, Comrade, if only you had followed the tactics of the Left Wing in the Third International; those tactics, that are nothing but the "pure" tactics of the Bolshevists in Russia, adapted to West-European (and North American) conditions!

If only, as stipulations and statutes for the Third International, you had proposed and carried through economic organisation in industrial organisations and workers' unions (into which, if need be, industrial unions on a shop floor basis might have been introduced), and political organisation in parties which reject parliamentarism!

Then you would in the first place have had, in all countries, absolutely firm kernels, parties that could really carry out the revolution, parties that would gradually have gathered the masses around them, through their own example, in their own country, and not through pressure from outside. Then you would have had economic organisations that would have annihilated the counter-revolutionary Trade Unions (syndicalist as well as free). And then with ONE stroke you would have cut off the way for all opportunists. For these can thrive only where there is plotting with the counter-revolution.

Then, likewise – and this is by far the most important point – you would have educated the workers into independent fighters to a very high degree, as far as it is possible in the present stage.

If you, Lenin, and you, Bukharin and Radek, had done this, had chosen these tactics, with your authority and experience, your strength and genius, and if you had helped us to eradicate the faults that cling to us as yet, and to our tactics, then we would have achieved a Third International that was perfectly firm internally, and unshakable externally, an International which would gradually have gathered the entire proletariat around it, through the force of its example, and which would have built Communism.

It is true that there are no tactics without defeat. But these would have suffered least defeat, and would most easily have recovered from it; they would have gone the quickest way, and would have won the quickest and surest victory. Yours lead to repeated defeat for the proletariat.

However, you have rejected this because, instead of conscious, steadfast fighters, you wanted partly or totally unconscious masses.

Conclusion

Finally I have to make a few observations regarding your last chapter: "Conclusions," perhaps the most important of your entire book. Again I was delighted with it, as long as I thought of the Russian revolution. But over and over again the thought came into my head: the tactics that are brilliant for Russia are bad here. They lead to defeat here.

You assert here, comrade (pp. 68-74), that in a certain stage of development the masses must be attracted, millions and millions of them. The propaganda for "pure" Communism, that collected the avant-garde, and educated it, suffices no longer in that stage. Now is the time, and next follow once again your opportunist methods that I have already refuted: taking advantage of "rifts," of petty-bourgeois elements, etc.

Comrade, this chapter is also completely wrong.

You judge as a Russian, not as an international Communist who knows real West-European capitalism.

Almost every word of this chapter, wonderful though it may be for the knowledge of your revolution, is wrong for big industrial capitalism, for the trusts and monopoly capitalism.

I will demonstrate this here: first in small matters.

Still Need for Propaganda.

You write about Communism in Western Europe.

"The vanguard of the West-European proletariat has been won" (p. 70). This is wrong, Comrade. "The period of propaganda is past" (p. 69). This is not true. "The proletarian vanguard has been won over ideologically." This is not so, Comrade. This stands in line (and it proceeds from the same mentality) with what I read in Bukharin, not long ago: "English capitalism is bankrupt." I also read in Radek similar fantasies, that were closer to astrology than astronomy. Nothing of this is true. Except for Germany, there is no vanguard anywhere yet. Neither in England, nor France, nor Belgium, nor Holland, nor, if I am well informed, in most of the Scandinavian countries. There are only a few "Eclaireurs," who do not agree yet about the course that must be followed (1). "The period of propaganda is past" is a terrible lie.

No, Comrade, this period is just beginning in Western Europe. There is no firm kernel anywhere as yet.

What we need here is such a kernel, hard as steel, clear as glass. And this is where we should begin herewith to build up a big organisation. In this respect we are here in the stage you were in 1903, or even before, in the Iskra period. Comrade, conditions here are far riper than we are, but that is no reason why we should let ourselves be carried away, to begin without a kernel!

---

1. The English Communists for instance, with regard to the most important matter of affiliation to the Labour Party.

For the time being we of Western Europe, the Communist parties in England, France, Belgium, Holland, Scandinavia, Italy, even the KAPD in Germany, must remain small, not because we want to, but because otherwise we cannot become strong.

An example: Belgium. Except for Hungary, before the revolution, there is no country where the proletariat is as corrupted by reformism as Belgium. If at this moment Communism should become a mass movement there (with parliamentarism, etc.), the vultures, the profiteers etc. of opportunism would swoop down on it immediately and drag it to destruction. And it is the same everywhere.

For that reason, because the Labour movement here is very weak as yet, and almost completely trapped in opportunism, because so far Communism is hardly anything, and must fight (on the questions of parliamentarism and the Trade Unions and on all others) until we attain the highest lucidity and clarity, until everything has been made theoretically as clear as possible.

A sect, therefore, says the Executive Committee. Certainly a sect, if that is what you want to call the kernel of a movement that conquers the world.

Comrade, there was a time when your movement, the Bolsheviks, was also small and insignificant. It was because it was small, and voluntarily remained so for a long time that it kept itself pure. And through this, and this exclusively it became powerful. We also want to proceed in this way.

This is a question of the utmost importance. Not only the West-European, but also the Russian revolution depends on this. Beware, Comrade! You know that Napoleon in trying to spread modern capitalism all over Europe was finally wrecked and had to make way for reaction, when he had arrived; where there was not only too much of the middle ages, but especially too little capitalism.

These, your minor assertions, are not true. I will now proceed to the bigger ones, to the most important of all you say: that now the time has come without propaganda to win the millions for "pure" Communism, through the opportunist policy you describe. Comrade, even if you were right in the small matters, if the Communist Parties here were actually strong enough, this would be utterly wrong from beginning to end. Pure propaganda for the new Communism, as I have often said already, will be necessary here in Western Europe, from the beginning of the revolution to the very end. Because (this point is of such importance that it has to be constantly repeated) it is the workers, the workers alone, who must bring Communism. Of the other classes they have nothing to expect, in any considerable measure, until the revolution is finished.

You say (p. 72): that period of the revolution has started in which we have the vanguard, and in which:

1. all class powers that are against us have become sufficiently disarranged, have fought sufficiently amongst themselves, have been sufficiently weakened by the struggle that surpasses their strength;

2. all vacillating, undecided elements, the petty-bourgeoisie, petty-bourgeois democracy, have been sufficiently unmasked before the people, have exposed themselves sufficiently through their bankruptcy.

Well, Comrade, this is Russian. In the Russian government body, which was rotten through and through, these were the conditions for the revolution.

In the modern, really big-capitalist states, however, the conditions will be altogether different. The big bourgeois parties will stand together in opposition to Communism, will not get disarranged, and the petty-bourgeoisie will stand by them. Not in an absolute sense, of course, but to such an extent that it has to determine our tactics.

Character of Western European Revolution.

In Western Europe we must expect a revolution that is a tenacious struggle on either side, with a firm organisation on the part of the bourgeoisie and the petty-bourgeoisie. The immense organisations of capitalism and of the workers prove this.

These, therefore, we have to organise likewise with the very best weapons, the best form of organisation, the best and strongest methods of fighting (not with weak ones).

It is here, and not in Russia, that the real struggle between capital and labour will be fought. Because here there is real capital.

Comrade, if you think that (from a tendency for theoretical purity), I exaggerate, just look at Germany. There you have an utterly bankrupt, almost desperate State. But all classes, big and petty bourgeois alike, as well as the peasant classes, stand firmly united against Communism. Thus it will be everywhere with us.

It is true that just at the end of the development of the revolution, when the most terrible crisis breaks out, when we are quite close to victory, the unity of the bourgeois classes will perhaps disappear, and some of the petty bourgeois and peasants will come to us. But what good is that to us? We must determine our tactics for the beginning and the course of the revolution.

Because this is so, and has to be so (because of the class relations and even more the relations of production) , the proletariat stands alone.

Because it stands alone, it can only triumph if it gains greatly in spiritual strength.

And as this is the only way it can triumph, propaganda for "pure" Communism is needed here until the very end (quite the contrary to Russia).

Without this propaganda, the West-European, and consequently the Russian proletariat, is lost.

And the same holds true of the Executive in Moscow.

Whilst I was writing these last few pages, the news came through that the International had adopted your tactics and those of the Executive. The West-European delegates have let themselves be dazzled by the brilliance of the Russian revolution. All right, we will take up the fight in the Third International.

We, Comrade, your old friends Pannekoek, Roland Holst, Rutgers and myself, truer than which you cannot find, on hearing of your West-European tactics, asked ourselves what could have caused them. Opinions differed greatly. The one said: the economic condition of Russia is so bad that, after all, it needs peace. For that reason, Comrade Lenin wants to gather around him as much power as possible: the Independents, Labour Party, etc., so that they may help him to obtain peace. The other said: he wishes to hasten the general European revolution. Therefore millions have to join. That is the reason for his opportunism.

I myself believe, as I have said before, that you misunderstand European conditions, the state of things.

However this may be, Comrade, and from what motives you may act, if you go on with these tactics, you will suffer the most terrible defeat, and you will lead the proletariat into the most terrible defeat.

For if you wish to save Russia, the Russian revolution, by means of these tactics, you collect non-Communist elements. You join them to us, the real Communists, whilst we do not as yet have a firm kernel! With this medley of dead Trade Unions, with a mass of half or quarter Communists, in which there is no solid kernel, you want to fight against the best organised capital in the world, with all the non-proletarian classes on its side. It goes without saying that in the battle this medley will fall apart, and the great mass will take flight.

Why German Workers must not be Defeated.

Comrade, a crushing defeat, of the German proletariat for instance, is the signal for a general attack on Russia.

If you wish to make the revolution here, with this hodgepodge of Labour Party and Independents, French Centre and the Italian Party, etc., and with these Trade Unions, the outcome cannot be otherwise. The governments will not even fear such a load of opportunists.

If however you form internally firm, radical groups, firm (though small) parties, then the government will fear these parties, as only these carry away the masses in great deeds in the revolution – as the Spartakus League has proved in the beginning – then the governments will have to release Russia, and finally, when the parties will thus, through these "pure" tactics, have grown powerful, victory will be ours. These our "Left" tactics, therefore, are the best; nay the only ones that bring salvation for us and for Russia alike.

Your tactics on the other hand are Russian. They were excellent in a country where an army of millions of poor peasants stood ready, and where there was a wavering, desperate middle class. Here they are no good.

I must finally refute your assertion and that of many of your associates, upon which I have already touched in the third chapter;

that the revolution in Western Europe can only begin after the lower, democratic layers of capitalism have been sufficiently shaken, neutralised or won.

This assertion also, in one of the most weighty questions of the revolution, proves once more that you consider everything from a purely East- European point of view. And this assertion is wrong.

For the proletariat in Germany and England is so numerous, so powerful through its organisation, that it can make the revolution, its beginning and development without, and in opposition to all these classes. And even that it must make the revolution, driven by sufferings in Germany.

And it can only do so, if it follows the right tactics, if it founds its organisation on a shop floor basis, and rejects parliamentarism; if only it strengthens the workers in this way!

We of the Left Wing, therefore, choose our tactics not only for the reason mentioned above, but especially also because the West-European proletariat, and in the first place the German and English proletariat, by itself alone, if only it grows conscious and united, is so immensely strong, that it can win in this simple manner. The Russian proletariat had to take roundabout ways, being too weak by itself, and it has done so brilliantly, in a manner far surpassing all that the world proletariat has ever achieved. But the West-European proletariat can triumph by the straight, clear road.

Thus also this assertion of yours has been refuted.

There remains one argument still to be refuted, one which I have read over and over again with the "Right" Communists, which I heard from the Russian Trade Union leader, Losovski, and which is to be found also with you: "The crisis will drive the masses to Communism, even if we retain the bad Trade Unions and parliamentarism." This is a very weak argument. For we have no idea how big the crisis is going to be. Will it be as deep in England and France as it is now in Germany? Secondly, this argument (the "mechanical argument of the Third International"), has proved how weak it is during the last six years. In Germany the misery during the last years of the war was terrible. The revolution did not break out. It was terrible in 1918 and 1919. The revolution did not triumph. The crisis in Hungary, Austria, the Balkans and Poland is terrible. The revolution did not come, or did not win, not even when the Russian armies were quite near. But in the third place the argument turns against yourself, for if the crisis should bring about the revolution in any case, the better "Left" tactics might be just as well adopted.

The examples of Germany, Hungary, Bavaria, Austria, Poland and the Balkans however, all prove that crisis and misery do not suffice. They have the most terrible economic crisis, and yet the revolution does not break out. There must be another cause yet, which brings the revolution about, and which, if it does not work, causes the delay, or the collapse of the revolution. This cause is the spirit of the masses. And it is your tactics, Comrade, which fail to sufficiently awaken the spirit of the masses in Western Europe, which does not sufficiently strengthen it, which leaves it as it was. In the course of writing I have pointed out that banking capital, the trusts, the monopolies and the West-European and North American state formed by them, and dependent on them, as they are, unite all bourgeois classes, big as well as small, into one whole against the revolution.

But this force, uniting society and the state against the revolution, goes even further. Banking capital itself organised the working class in a previous period, in the period of evolution, against the revolution: educating, uniting and organising them. And in what way? In the Trade Unions (Syndicalist as well as free), and in the social-democratic parties. By forcing them to fight only for reforms, capital turned these Trade Unions and Labour parties into counter-revolutionary forces for the maintenance of the State and society. Because of big capital, Trade Unions and Labour parties became props of capitalism. As, however, these organisations consist of workers, and of almost the majority of workers, and as the revolution cannot be made without the workers, these organisations must be destroyed before the revolution can succeed. And how are they to be destroyed? By changing their spirit. And their spirit can only be changed by making the spirit of the members independent to the utmost degree. And this can be done only by replacing the Trade unions with industrial unions and workers' unions, and by abolishing parliamentarism in the Labour parties. And your tactics prevent this.

It is true that German, French and Italian capitalism is bankrupt. Or rather: these capitalist States are bankrupt. The capitalists themselves, their economic and political organisations, maintain themselves and their profits, dividends and new capital are still huge. Only, however, by an extension of the circulation of paper by the State. If the German, French and Italian States fall, the capitalists fall likewise.

Crisis is Nearing.

The crisis approaches with an iron necessity. If prices rise, strike waves rise as well; if they fall, the army of the unemployed increases. Misery is spreading all over Europe, and hunger is approaching. Moreover, the world is full of new fuel. The conflict, the new revolution, is drawing near. But how will it end? Capitalism is still powerful. Germany, Italy, France and Eastern Europe are not the whole world. And in Western Europe, North America and the British Dominions, for some time to come, capitalism will hold together all classes against the proletariat. The issue therefore to a very great extent depends on our tactics and on our organisation. And your tactics are wrong.

Here in Western Europe there is only one kind of tactics: those of the Left Wing, that tells the proletariat the truth, and does not blind it with illusions. Those that, even though it may take a long time, forge the only effective weapons – the industrial organisations (uniting these into one whole), and the originally small, but pure and firm kernels, the Communist parties. Those tactics, moreover, that spread these organisations over the entire proletariat.

This has to be like this, not because we of the Left Wing want it, but because the relations of production, class relations, demand it.

At the conclusion of my exposition, I will draw them up in a concise survey, so that the worker may see everything clearly for himself.

In the first place, I imagine, there follows from it a clear image of the causes of our tactics (a clear survey of the motives of our tactics), and the tactics themselves: banking capital dominates the whole world. Ideologically and materially it keeps the gigantic proletariat in the deepest slavery, and unites all bourgeois classes. Consequently the gigantic masses must rise and proceed to act for themselves. This is only possible through industrial organisations and the abolition of parliamentarism in the revolution.

Secondly, I will summarise the tactics of the Left Wing, and those of the Third International in a few phrases, so that the difference between your tactics and those of the Left Wing become clearly and absolutely obvious, and so that if your tactics lead to the greatest debacle, as they probably will, the workers will not lose courage, but might see there are other tactics.

The Third International believes that the West-European revolution will proceed together according to the laws and tactics of the Russian revolution.

The Left Wing believes that the West-European revolution will make and follow its own laws.

The Third International believes that the West-European revolution will be able to make compromises and alliances with petty-bourgeois and small peasant, and even with big bourgeois parties.

The Left Wing believes this is impossible.

The Third International believes that in Western Europe during the revolution there will be "rifts" and scissions between the bourgeois, petty-bourgeois and small peasant parties.

The Left Wing believes that the bourgeois and petty-bourgeois parties will form one united front until the end of the revolution.

The Third International underestimates the power of West-European and North American capital.

The Left Wing makes its tactics conform to this great power.

The Third International does not recognise the power of banking capital, the big capital which unites all bourgeois classes.

The Left Wing on the contrary bases its tactics on this unifying power.

As the Third International does not believe in the fact that in Western Europe the proletariat will stand alone, it neglects the mental development of this proletariat; which in every respect is still deeply entangled in bourgeois ideology; and chooses tactics which leave slavery and subjection to bourgeois ideas unmolested and intact.

Left-Winger to Free Workers' Minds.

The Left Wing chooses its tactics in such a way that in the first place the mind of the workers is liberated.

As the Third International does not found its tactics on freeing the mind, nor on the unity of all bourgeois and petty-bourgeois parties, but on compromises and "rifts"; it leaves the old Trade Unions intact, trying to unite them with the Third International.

As the Left Wing strives above all for freeing the mind, and believes in the unity of the bourgeois parties, it realises that the Trade Unions must be destroyed, and that the proletariat needs better weapons.

The same motives induce the Third International to support parliamentarism.

The same motives also induce the Left Wing to abolish parliamentarism.

The Third International leaves the condition of slavery such as it was in the Second.

The Left Wing wishes to change it from below upward; it seizes the evil at the root.

As the Third International does not believe that in the first place the liberation of minds is needed in Western Europe, nor that all bourgeois parties will be one in the revolution, it collects masses around it, without inquiring whether they are really Communist, without determining its tactics, on the supposition that they are – as long as it gets the masses.

The Left Wing wishes in all countries to form parties consisting exclusively of Communists, and determines its tactics accordingly. Through the example of these originally small parties, the majority of the proletariat, and therefore the masses, will be brought to Communism.

To the Third International, then, the masses in Western Europe are a means.

To the Left Wing they are the aim.

Through these tactics (which were quite right in Russia), the Third International employs leader-politics.

The Left Wing, on the other hand, employs mass politics.

Through these tactics the Third International is leading not only the West-European, but also the Russian revolution, into ruin.

The Left Wing on the other hand, through its tactics, leads the world proletariat towards victory.

And, finally, I will gather my statements into a few theses, so that the workers who must strive for themselves to gain a clear insight into those tactics, may have them before their eyes in a concise, surveyable form. They have to be read, of course, in the light of the above exposition.

1. The tactics of the West-European revolution must be different from those of the Russian revolution.

2. For here the proletariat stands alone.

3. Here the proletariat must make the revolution all by itself, against all other classes.

4. The importance of the proletarian masses, therefore, is relatively greater, and that of the leaders smaller than in Russia.

5. Consequently, here the proletariat must have the very best weapons for the revolution.

6. The Trade Unions being insufficient weapons, they must be replaced or changed into industrial organisations, that are united into one league.

7. As the proletariat must make the revolution all alone, without help, it has to rise very high morally as well as spiritually. It is better therefore not to use parliamentarism in the revolution.

Marx had learnt from the Paris Commune the proletariat cannot use or take over the bourgeois State for the revolution. Thus the "Left Wing" has learnt from the Russian, German, Hungarian, from the World Revolution, that the proletariat cannot use the old Socialist parties, nor the old Trade Unions for the revolution.

With fraternal greetings,

H. Gorter

Why We Need the Fourth Communist Workers' International

"The Workers' Dreadnought", October 22nd, 1921

The post-war situation of the international workers' movement is distinguished from the pre-war period by certain fundamental changes.

Through the war a great world economic crisis has increased the tension between capital and labour to breaking point. The general disruption of the capitalist system of production has lowered enormously the standard of living of the world proletariat. Nevertheless, the working class of the entire world, without exception, undoubtedly remains content to better its condition, if it can, within the capitalist system, by the old pre-war methods. Especially in the countries which are directly affected by the war has the vicious and fallacious running round in a circle, from which there is no escape, been developed. It is clearly proven here that every apparent increase in wages is automatically nullified through a corresponding rise in the price of commodities on the one side, and on the other, through the greater output of the paper money press, which causes a fallacious depreciation in the value of money. The rise in the price of commodities, which is simultaneous with the depreciation in the money value, is naturally followed by fresh wage demands, and thus the vicious circle continues.

This situation, so unbearable for the exploited classes, can only be altered by the destruction of the capitalist system and the establishment of a Communist, system of production and distribution.

Whilst the policy of social reform was once an historic necessity to raise the condition of the working class, as a preparation for undertaking the final struggle for political and economic power; to-day social reformist tactics are proved to be wholly illusory. To pursue them further will cause ever-increasing misery to the proletariat, a misery which as it grows will stimulate their revolutionary energies.

The development sketched here in outline, has called forth, within the working class itself, far-reaching changes, which have led it far from its position before the world war. The outstanding characteristic of the epoch of the Second International is the organisational unity of the workers' movement. Social Democracy was, in effect, the united political organisation of the proletariat, whilst the Trade Unions fulfilled the same function on the economic field. This organisational unity bound together political conceptions which were diametrically opposed. Thus the German Social Democracy united the Revolutionary Wing of Liebknecht, Rosa Luxemburg and Mehring with the revisionist tendency of Bernstein, Heine, David, etc., and between these two extremes was the famous Marxist Centre. The uniting within one party of tendencies which were as the poles apart, when regarded historically, is seen to have been possible only because, during the period of the Second International, social reform and revolution did not confront each other as dialectical antitheses. Both principles formed then a united whole in the class-war. That is the real reason why it was possible to have a united political organisation, as represented by social democracy in the pre-war period.

The characteristic phenomenon of the post-war workers' movement is the organisational disruption on the political and economic field. The splitting of the organisationally united framework is a clear proof that the political oppositions within the working class have acquired quite a different significance from that they presented during the Second International period. The mass of the proletariat today groups itself round the two poles: Social Reform, and Revolution. The position today differs from that of the pre-war period in that these two poles represent absolute opposites, which mutually exclude each other.

The policy of Social Reform is synonymous today with a Reformist policy. The leaders of Reformism, as in the pre-war period, are the Trade Unions; but equally so today are those parties which are working in league with the Trade Unions. The chief aim of the Trade Unions is to reconstruct Capitalism. This aim is quite clearly formulated by them. Therefore, for them, alliance is only possible with parties which stand for the reconstruction of Capitalism and accept as a basis the political and economic union of the bourgeoisie and the proletariat.

In this sense the Moscow International works quite openly with the Amsterdam Trade Union International and the "Two and a Half International". To most of the sections adhering to the Third International, this is neither repugnant nor surprising, because they have remained inherently the same Social Democratic Parties which they were before their baptism in the holy water of Communism. The only new circumstance is that the language as well as the composition of the Third International can no longer be distinguished from that of Social Democracy. No longer will it set aside any manifestoes as opportunist; the call to participation in the reconstruction of Capitalism resounds ever more clearly as the official Moscow policy.

In Germany the participation of the Communist Party in the united front presented by those sections of the proletariat which have made common cause with bourgeois democracy for the protection of the capitalist Republic, speaks in such unmistakable language that every proletarian must notice in which direction the Communist Party has turned. This is perhaps more clearly apparent in the abandonment of the tactics of opposition to the reactionary Trade Unions, on the part of the German Communist Party. The deal by which the revolutionary district executive of the Halle Metalworkers was united by the Communist Party with the Central Union, from which it had seceded, was not exactly honourable. In fact it was a suspension of the fight against the Amsterdam International and a direct participation in the reconstruction of Capitalism under the wing of Amsterdam. Today the Moscow International finds itself in tow to the Amsterdam International, which means that it is actually in tow to the international bourgeoisie. The more Russia develops towards Capitalism, the more apparent will be the bourgeois character of the Third International.

Therefore we must admit that, regarded from an international standpoint, there is at present no organisation capable and willing of stepping forth as the instrument of the revolutionary world proletariat in the struggle against Capitalism and its adherents in the proletarian camp.

International Capitalism, aided by the Trade Unions, will make desperate attempts to overcome the present economic crisis. The overcoming of the economic crisis is largely dependent upon the opening of the Russian market to West European capital. The English and German capitalist groups especially are working to this end.

As a significant new sign, the tendency of the capitalist Great Powers to come to an understanding amongst themselves must be emphasised. In spite of the deep-rooted opposition of economic interests between Britain and America, Britain finds herself compelled to avoid every open conflict with the great trusts across the Atlantic. The same is true of England and France, and of America and Japan.

The national antagonisms within the sphere of world capitalism pale ever more and more. The economic and political collapse in the world standard of values rises as a threatening spectre before the proletariat of all countries. The Imperialist conflict of the capitalist Great Powers against each other is sunk in the class-war of international capitalism against the world proletariat. The withdrawal of Russia as a factor in the world revolution has completely altered the whole situation. A united bourgeois front for the reconstruction of Capitalism in conjunction with the Amsterdam Trade Unions and the Third International, has become an accomplished fact.

The revolutionary working class of the whole world stands powerless before the situation. It has no class-war organisation which would be capable and willing to lead the revolutionary struggle aiming at the dictatorship of the proletariat and Communism by proletarian methods. The longer the situation remains which secures to Capitalism an unbounded playground for the reconstruction of capitalist economy, so much harder will it be for the proletariat to maintain its defensive position towards the bourgeoisie and the bourgeois position.

The sooner an international centre comes into being, which will incorporate the interests of the proletarian revolution, so much sooner will the fall of the Third International take place.

A crystallised kernel must be formed to which those elements and groups which are opposed to the Moscow International and are comprised of what is known as "Left" Communism.

If the construction of a Communist Workers' International does not take place at the right moment, we must expect those organisations in all countries which now stand for the platform of the Communist Workers' Party of Germany to fall back to the level of the Third International.

The Conference of the Communist Workers' Party of Germany (the K.A.P.D.) has shown that it understands the signs of the times, and is willing to undertake the mighty task to be accomplished in the interests of Communism and the World Revolution.

PART TWO
Anton Pannekoek

The Labor Movement and Socialism

International Socialist Review, July 1908

The relation of labor unions to the Socialist movement is in many countries the subject of sharp differences of opinion, even of bitter strife. The situation is by no means everywhere the same. In England, for example, after the break-up of the Chartist political movement in 1848 the union movement increased greatly and became a mighty organization of the workingmen. But this great body of workers remained indifferent to Socialism, or even inimical to it, and the Socialist party remained a small sect. In America the labor movement developed according to the English pattern. In Germany and Belgium, on the contrary, the situation is exactly reversed. There the Socialist party grew mightily in the first place; then the workers, who had learned how to conduct the fight on the political field, began to struggle for better conditions against individual employers. On this account the unions remained in these countries closely connected with the Socialist party; in Belgium, in fact, they are an organic part of the Socialist movement. Here they are, however, comparatively weak, and it is to be expected that as they increase in strength they will make themselves more independent.

This division is imposed by the different objects of the political and labor union struggles. The Socialist party holds to a great and far-reaching purpose; a purpose not immediately understood by everyone; a purpose which, in fact, is often misunderstood and therefore has to meet opposition, prejudice and hatred which can be overcome only through extended educational propaganda. The objective of the unions, on the other hand, is an immediate one, the securing of higher wages and shorter hours. This is instantly intelligible to everyone; does not demand deep convictions, but appeals rather to immediate interest. On this account quite undeveloped workers must not be hindered from joining the unions because of their prejudice against a world-overturning force like Socialism. As soon as the unions attempt to take in the great mass of the workers they must be absolutely independent. Of course a friendly relation to the Socialist party can still be maintained.

This is the situation in Germany. The unions are independent organizations; they are "neutral," i.e., they ask no questions as to the religious or political opinions of their members. They remain, however, constantly in friendly touch with the Socialist party, even if now and then a little friction does occur. "Party and union are one," is the oft quoted expression of a prominent union leader; this is taken for granted because of the fact that the party members and the great body of union adherents are the same persons, the same workingmen.

The need of having unions to improve the immediate situation of the workers and the advantages which grow out of these need not be examined. But the goal of the working class is the complete extermination of capitalism. Have the unions any part in this struggle for the complete liberation of the proletariat? Before this question can be answered we must make a closer investigation into the general conditions of the struggle for the freedom of the workers.

Why does the great body of workingmen still permit itself to be ruled and exploited by the capitalists? Why are they not in a position to drive the minority of exploiters from power? Because they are an unorganized, undisciplined, individualistic and ignorant mass. The majority is impotent because it consists of a divided crowd of individuals each one of whom wishes to act according to his own impulse, regard his own interests, and in addition has no understanding of our social system. It lacks organization and knowledge. The minority, the ruling class, on the contrary, is strong because it possesses both organization and knowledge. Not only does it have in its service scholars and men of learning; it controls also a strong organization, the state administration. The army of officials, government underlings, law-givers, judges, representatives, politicians and soldiers works like a gigantic machine which instantly suppresses any attack on the existing order; a machine against which every individual is powerless and by which, if he opposes it, he is crushed like a troublesome insect; a machine which, indeed, can easily shatter in a struggle even a great organization of workers. In this machine each works as a part of the whole: in the working class each man acts for himself or a small group. No wonder that the few, through their superior strength, rule the majority with ease.

But things are already changing. Economic development is always producing greater machines, more gigantic factories, more colossal capitalizations. It gathers ever greater bodies of laborers about these machines, forces them into organized trade under the command of capital, robs them of their personal and national distinctions and takes from them the possibility of personal success. But incidentally it suggests to them the thought of organization, of union of their forces, as the only means of improving their position and opposing the overpowering might of capital. Economic development thus brings forth the labor movement, which begins the class-struggle against capital.

The object of the labor movement is to increase the strength of the proletariat to the point at which it can conquer the organized force of the bourgeoisie and thus establish its own supremacy. The power of the working class rests, in the first place, upon its members and upon the important role which it plays in the process of production. It constitutes an increasingly large majority of the population. Production proceeds upon a constantly increasing scale, and so is carried on more and more by wage-workers; and the relations of its branches grows constantly more complex. Under these circumstances workingmen find it possible through the strike to bring our whole social life to a standstill. In order that they may be in a position to use this great power in the right way the workers must come to a consciousness of their situation and master an understanding of, and insight into, our social system. They must be class-conscious, i. e., clearly recognize the clash of interests between themselves and the capitalists. And they must have sufficient intelligence to find the right methods of prosecuting the class-struggle and reject the wrong ones.

Enlightenment, the spreading of knowledge, is therefore one of the mightiest and most important weapons of the labor movement; this is the immediate purpose of the Socialist propaganda. In the third place, means must be found to turn knowledge into deeds, to apply intelligence to action. To do this we need an organization in which the powers of the individual are joined in a single will and thereby fused into a common social force. The outer form of organization is not the main thing, but the spirit which holds the organization together. Just as the grains of sand are held together by a cement and thus the mass of them becomes a heavy stone, so must the individuals be cemented together so that the organization will not fly asunder at the first opposition, but rather will conquer all opposition like a mighty mass. This immaterial, spiritual cement is the discipline which leads the individual to subordinate his own will to that of the whole and to place his entire strength at the disposal of the community. It is not the giving up of one's own views, but the recognition of the fact that united action is necessary and that the minority cannot expect the majority to conform to its notions — a recognition which has become a powerful motive for action.

The first of the three factors which constitute the strength of the working class will be increasingly developed by economic evolution independently of our will. The further development of the other two is the task of the labor movement. All our working and striving is devoted to this purpose: to improve the knowledge, the class-consciousness, the organization, the discipline, of the working class. Only when these are sufficiently developed can we conquer the most powerful organization of the ruling class, the state.

Now what are the respective parts played in this development of working class power by the political party and the labor union? Through sermons, speeches and theoretic instruction we can never call into being organization and discipline — no, not even social intelligence and class-consciousness. The worth of theoretic instruction lies in the fact that it explains and illuminates practical experience, brings it to clear consciousness; but it cannot serve as a substitute for this experience. Only through practice, practice in the struggle, can the workers acquire that understanding of theoretic teaching and those intellectual and moral qualities which will make their power great.

It is generally known that in western Europe it has been the politico-parliamentary activity which has chiefly contributed to the tremendous increase of the Socialist movement and everywhere given strength to the Social Democratic parties. What is the meaning of this? That the political struggle has given a mighty impetus to the class-consciousness, the insight, the group-feeling, of the hitherto unconscious, unrelated workers. The representatives of the workers took a stand in parliament against the government and the bourgeois parties, tore from their faces the masks of guardians of "the general welfare", revealed them as expressions of bourgeois interests inimical to the workers, and through suggestions for the improvement of the conditions of the laborers forced them to show their true characters; by these means they enlightened the people as to the class character of the state and the rulers. The critique which they carried on in debate with the mouthpieces of the bourgeoisie and the capitalist system penetrated through the papers to the uttermost corners of the land and roused to reflection those who otherwise remain untouched by public gatherings. The careful following of parliamentary struggles, of the speeches of their own representatives and of their opponents, developed to a high degree the political intelligence of the workers and increased their understanding of social phenomena. Herein lies the significance of the political struggle for the increase of the power of the working class; the totally unconscious are shaken up and induced to think; their class-consciousness awakes and they join the class organizations of the proletariat; the already class-conscious workingmen become better and better instructed and their knowledge becomes more thorough.

Just as important is the activity connected with labor union struggle. The effect of this conflict is to build up and strengthen the workingmen's organization. Through the efforts of the union to improve the conditions of labor increasing numbers of workers who before kept themselves at a distance are aroused and brought into the organization. The most effective recruiting force, it is generally known, is not the designed propaganda carried on through meetings and tracts, but the influence of strikes and lock-outs. The chief significance of these struggles, however, lies in the development of discipline and mutual fidelity. This becomes tough as steel only when it has been tempered in the fire of conflict. The suppression of egotism, the surrender of the individual to the whole, the sacrifice of the individual interest for the organization, can be learned and thoroughly ingrained only in struggle. Experience of the fact that all together suffer defeat if the individual lacks the necessary feeling of solidarity, that on the other hand victory is the reward of unwavering co-operation, beats into everyone this necessary discipline. It is thus the labor unions which weld the scattered individualistic workers into powerful units, teach them to act unitedly as a body, and produce among them the highest working class virtue, solidarity.

In addition the labor union struggle contributes to the knowledge of the workers. It is in this conflict that most of them learn the ABC of Socialism, the opposition of interests between workingmen and employers. Here they can get hold of this fundamental fact of capitalistic society, which appears much less clearly in the political fight. On this account the unions have often been called the preparatory schools of Socialism; they might be better called elementary schools, for the real elementary principles that one learns in the labor struggle. Of course this elementary knowledge of the opposition of interests between employees and employers is not adequate to an understanding of our social system; one who knows nothing more will be nonplussed and without resource when he confronts the more complex relations, the role of the other classes, of the office-holders, of the state, for example, and other political and ideological phenomena.

On the other hand, the political struggle has an essential significance for the organizations of the working class. The union organizations always have their limitations; they include only members of a particular craft, and so develop with the strong solidarity of their fellow craftsmen their guild spirit, their isolation, yes, often an unfriendly jealously of other crafts. This narrowness is swept away by the political struggle. In politics class stands against class. There the delegates of labor speak not as representatives of the carpenters or the miners; they do not even represent the wage-workers exclusively, but the whole body of those exploited by capital. Their opponents are not representatives of definite groups of employers, but of the whole owning class; they fight in parliament against bank capital, colonial capital, land capital, just as much as against all exploiters. Therefore the political conflict extends the view, the intelligence and also the sympathies beyond the narrow circle of the craft interests of the labor union. Where the political party is strong all workers of the most varied trades feel themselves brothers; their solidarity is no longer limited by the boundaries of their crafts, and their labor organizations appear to them as parts, as branches, as battalions in a single great labor army. In Germany, where the political organization preceded the labor union, the guild spirit was unable to develop itself so strongly as, e. g., in England.

The relation between political party and union is often represented as though the political movement were to bring about the destruction of capitalism, and the union to effect the improvement of the laborer's condition within the capitalist system; as though the political party were naturally revolutionary and the union naturally reformatory. This may be in harmony with the apparent practice in many lands; but in France, on the contrary, the unions regard themselves as the revolutionary organizations and the political party as a bourgeois creation with merely temporary reformatory functions. In reality the truth is that both are at once revolutionary and reformatory: that is to say, they both carry on the present struggle for direct improvement and both have great significance in relation to the revolutionary transformation of society.

In the class-struggle the conflict must always concern itself with immediate, practical objects. What are the bones of contention in parliament? The introduction of Socialism? One may agitate for a purpose lying far in the future, but cannot carry on an immediate fight for it. The actual fight turns about definite legislative proposals; about social reforms, laws for the protection of laborers, contraction or expansion of the rights of labor, laws in the interest of particular capitalist groups, or measures of taxation in regard to which there is a collision of class interests. Every article of a law becomes the crux of a struggle between the representatives of labor and the bourgeoisie. labor gains only now and then a direct advantage, a favourable legal enactment; but always an indirect one, the enlightenment of the masses as to the nature of society and the state.

The difference between this and the union struggle for direct improvement — of the conditions of labor — lies in the fact that in the political fight more general interests and considerations come into question. Therefore the arguments brought to bear reach a higher level. From momentary questions the opponents reach out to remote purposes; eventually their deepest most general convictions, their world-views, come into conflict. Socialist speakers utilize every particular case to make an attack on the whole capitalist system; their opponents answer with attempts at criticism of Socialist teaching. So the ultimate objective of the proletarian struggle always appears behind the momentary clash, and we always emphasize the fact that this clash gains in significance from its relation to this ultimate objective. So it comes about that apparently the political struggle is carried on in the interests of Socialism, and the union struggle in the interests of reform. And yet both are for reform, for the improvement of the condition and status of labor and against their deterioration. Both of them effect, as we showed above, a steady increase in the power of the working class; pave the way, therefore, for the conquest of political power by the proletariat.

In both there comes about in an analogous manner a limited conception of their function, in that all remote purposes and general interests are sacrificed to the achievement of an immediate reform. On the political field this conception takes the form of a neglect of the class-struggle, a political alliance with the bourgeois parties in a bloc, a strife for votes as a main object; this constitutes the tendency within the Socialist movement which is called reformist or revisionist. The belief that through it we can accomplish more reforms usually proves fallacious, and in addition the revolutionary result of political activity, the enlightenment and organization of labor, usually fails of accomplishment. This tendency can prosper only under underdeveloped conditions such as obtain among small capitalists or land-holders, conditions under which the opposition of classes is not sharply defined — and even there not for any great length of time.

The reformist tendency is much more persistent among the unions. Where on account of particular circumstances the unions have been successful in improving the labor conditions there may easily develop in their ranks a self-satisfied, bigoted conservatism; they give up the thought of a vigorous campaign against capitalism and surrender themselves to the stupor of the "community of interests between capital and labor;" they neglect further enlightenment, isolate their organizations like guilds, look with scorn on the miserable, unorganised mass of sacrifices to capitalism, and become small bourgeois, lacking anything like revolutionary feeling. The classical examples of this are furnished by the English and American trades-unions. In such a labor movement, in distinction from a reformist political movement, the very name of the Socialist enlightenment is proscribed. Under such circumstances a better view of things becomes effective only with great difficulty and as the result of the most painful lessons of experience. In most countries, naturally, the conservative, reformist tendencies are most powerful in the unions; while the political party, on the contrary, represents more energetically the revolutionary standpoint. But the opposite is also possible. Where the Socialist party loses itself too deep in the quagmire of bourgeois parliamentary there awakes in the workers a native, primitive class feeling, a disgust at the coquetting with the representatives of the bourgeoisie. Then they repudiate the whole fight on the political field as a quarrel of ambitious politicians which can only compromise the class-struggle; and they come to place their only trust in the natural organizations of the working class, the unions. So in France, chiefly as a result of the bloc policy and Millerandism, there has arisen a revolutionary unionism which advocates the general strike as the only weapon whereby labor can accomplish the overthrow of capitalism.

The goal of the labor movement, the conquest of political power, indicates in itself that its attainment can be accomplished only by the working class organized as a political party. Repeatedly has the idea been presented, especially by the revisionists, that this conquest can be brought about in a simple, peaceful, parliamentary manner. In every election we poll an increased number of votes, a constantly increasing number of voters is being converted to our views; and when at last we have won the majority of the people we shall have — universal, equal suffrage being taken for granted — the majority in parliament will make laws according to our principles. But this beautiful idyll goes to smash the moment we take into account the restrictions upon suffrage which the bourgeois parties are in a position to put through so long as they are still in control of the majority. It goes without saying that the ruling class will not allow itself to be so easily discarded. It will attempt to assert itself against us with all the weapons at its command; its wealth, and above all its actual control of the political administration, the bureaucracy, the army and the newspapers, give it a tremendous power; so long as it has a majority in the law-giving bodies it can by legal methods do away with the popular rights which are dangerous to it. Experience has shown that in defense of its privileges it is not inclined either in Europe and America to respect recognized rights. In the face of these facts the workers will be forced to call into the field every power which they possess.

In this final struggle for the mastery — which will not be a single battle, but a long war with many ups and downs of victory and defeat — the unions will play a part not inferior to that of the Socialist party. Or, to put it more clearly, the political and the union movement will come together in this conflict. The workers must present themselves as a single, strongly united class with a definite political purpose — that is, as a political party. They must at the same time come into action as a mass organization, i. e., lead into the field their unions and make use of their union weapon, the strike, for political purposes; they must act as a body against the power of the state. In the mass strike the two proletarian methods become one: political understanding and union discipline are here like the thinking head and the strong arm of an individual combatant.

The more the great body of workers take part in the war on capitalism, the more will labor union conflicts become social cataclysms, great political events; and thus the unions will be forced to take part in the political struggle. In these great struggles the old methods of parliamentary and labor union diplomacy will be found inadequate; the cleverness of sharp leaders and versatile spokesmen will be overshadowed by the power of the masses themselves. In the persons of the leaders, who develop according to the particular demands of each form of action, the political and union movements are different; in the persons who constitute the masses behind the leaders they are identical. Thus where the mass of the workers themselves come into action the dividing line between the two methods of struggle disappears; they march upon the field of battle to a single, undivided warfare against capitalism, armed with the class-consciousness, the discipline, the intelligence and the power of action gained in all previous conflicts; the union constitutes their organization; Socialism, their political intelligence.

The German Revolution - First Stage

Workers Dreadnought, 24 May 1919

The logical result of the collapse of German Imperialism following the military defeat, was the revolution.

On November 4th the revolt in Kiel occurred. The ferment manifested itself first among the sailors. Rumours of revolt among the sailors were heard during the past year, and the Independent Social Democrats defended themselves against the accusations of complicity. Now it broke out anew, stronger and more general, "by mistake" as the *Vossiche Zeitung* said. Revolutions often occur through such mistakes – the conviction amongst the sailors that the fleet was ordered out to hopeless combat.

The sailors organised a council, arrested their officers, hoisted the red flag, and presented their demands to the Government. The social-patriot, Noske, arriving in Kiel, attempted to stop them but in vain.

On November 5th the movement extended to Hamburg, where the dock workers declared for a sympathetic strike; traffic ceased and the soldiers joined the revolution. Within the next few days the movement spread to Bremen, Wilhelmshaven, Lubeck, and throughout the northern regions generally, while Wolff's Bureau sent out vague reports of the revolt and the prediction that it would be quickly suppressed. In Berlin the intrigue of new ministries continued. Max von Baden disappeared, the Social Democratic Party presented an ultimatum to the Government and *Vorwaerts* entreated the workers to remain "calm" – counter-revolutionary to the last. Meanwhile, the revolution continued to spread; in Cologne, Munich, Stuttgart, throughout Germany.

Everywhere Workers' and Soldiers' Councils sprang into being and imprisoned the officers and officials of the old regime, except those who declared their willingness to assist the revolution. Everywhere the new Republic was proclaimed, kings and princes abdicated and disappeared, and, finally, on November 9th, Emperor Wilhelm abdicated. Berlin, which remained calm until the last, went over to the revolution, the Soldiers' and Workers' Council took control without bloodshed, and the police of the old regime disappeared from the streets. The movement extended to the Western front, and Wilhelm was forced to flee from the General Staff Headquarters at Spa to the Netherlands.

With scarcely any resistance, in one assault, the revolution was victorious. This proves that the old system was already crumbling and had lost the entire sympathy of the masses, whose sufferings had reached their climax through the war and whose fear of the old regime was banished through the military defeat. This inflammable situation, where one spark spread the flames everywhere, enabled the secret preparations of the groups of the Independents and the extreme left for an armed uprising to break into action, and thus leaders sprang up everywhere to take command. So with the fall of German Imperialism also fell the political form wherein it functioned: the absolutistic, feudal, militaristic, police state was replaced by the democratic republic.

Through its rapidity and unanimity the revolution rested on the surface of civil society and could not as yet penetrate into the depth of the great masses. For those who accomplished it, the revolution, as all modern revolutions, is a proletarian revolution. But in its objects and results it is, as yet, only a purely political, and, therefore, a bourgeois revolution. This is evident from the fact that the social-patriotic leaders, Ebert and Scheidemann, were selected to function as the heads of the provisional government.

It seems at first glance unaccountable that the masses, driven to desperation on account of the war and its horrors should overthrow and expel those responsible for the war, and, at the same time allow their accomplices, who always supported the war policy, to take the helm. But this is simply the result of political incompetence and traditional adherence to the old Social Democracy. The four years of war, through the pressure of the battlefield and the activity of the censor, made political development, except in small groups, impossible. The masses have destroyed the machinery that crushed them, they have won their political liberty, and now the political development, the orientation of what they further desire, can be started. They are still impressed with the naïve illusions of the first days of the revolution – even as in Paris in 1848; these later revolutions must first go through the development of former revolutions – the illusions of the people's unity, of liberty and democracy.

The various denominations and reflections of these fantastic illusions: we speak of the People's Republic, the rulers are called the People's representatives, we pass motions against all discord and dissension. The reality of society, the class distinction of bourgeoisie and proletariat seems to have disappeared. As this reality again becomes apparent the class struggle will burst forth anew. It will be sharp and violent in Germany because both the bourgeoisie and the proletariat are strong, their class consciousness is forceful and production is highly developed. This will be the next stage of the revolution; it is even now developing.

How are these contending forces arrayed?

In normal times the bourgeoisie rules through its powerful and perfectly organised state apparatus, whereas the masses are divided into separate groups and are thus powerless. Revolutions occur when the masses are spontaneously inspired by *one* will and thus find power in their unity. New individuals take the helm, different forms of government come, but then the masses resume their daily tasks, the inspiring fire of *one* powerful will evaporates, they again fall apart as individuals and groups, while the bourgeois apparatus that remained and was deprived of its power only temporarily, retakes its old position unopposed by any organised force, and again becomes the stable organisation of rule. So, through the storms of the revolution class rule grows and becomes stronger as the experience of the revolution teaches it to pretend, to adopt the external forms of democracy, the dress of people's rule – the rulers change but the rule *over* the masses remains. To destroy this rule it is necessary to break the old government's organisation, the old bureaucracy, and to strengthen the temporary organisation of the masses into lasting power. This happened in Paris in 1871 by the Commune, and in Russia in November by the Soviets.

In Germany the workers have created such an organisation, the same as took place in Russia, in the formation of Workers' and Soldiers' Councils. These councils gave the revolution a direct power which led to its initial speedy victory. They are the new instrument of power for the masses, the organisation of the proletarian masses as against the organisation of the bourgeoisie. They do not, as yet, know what they want, but they are there – not their programme but their very existence has revolutionary significance. A revolutionary government which wishes to be the organ of the Socialist proletariat should commence now to remove the old functionaries and abolish their functions.

The government of Ebert, Scheidemann and Haase has done the contrary. It has attempted to force the Soldiers' Councils into a subordinate commission of advice and to restore the disciplinary powers of the officers which has resulted, in many places, in strong resistance and refusal by the soldiers. It has maintained the old bureaucracy and allowed it to continue its rule; it has done the same as every bourgeois party does when it assumes control – taken for itself the best positions and left all else in *status quo ante*. It has retained the old generals in command of the army and has made no attempt to further revolutionary propaganda amongst the soldiers. Thus, by allowing the apparatus of the ruling class to remain intact it openly encourages the counter-revolution. Already the bureaucrats openly denounce the "government of dilettantes", the generals at the front order the red flag hauled down, and every reaction is encouraged.

The bourgeoisie is entirely satisfied with this government, especially since it announced that no change will be made in property rights and that the banks will not be nationalised. The reason for these announcements is that the government is trying to rely upon the whole population, upon the workers and the bourgeoisie alike, thus, upon the co-operation of the classes it hopes to be the government of the "continued God's peace". This is a reflection of the unconsciousness of the masses, and will become increasingly impossible with the more forceful awakening of the class struggle.

For the time being the government swings between the classes, it has conservative deeds for the bourgeoisie and revolutionary phrases for the workers – because the bourgeoisie is alertly class conscious and not easily defrauded, while the workers are not yet fully awakened. The first part, the appeasement of the middle classes is taken care of by Ebert and Scheidemann, while the nice Radical speechmaking is the task of the so-called "Left Wing", the Independents: Dittman and Barth, who were included in the government for this reason.

The majority Socialists lack confidence in Socialism and in the ability of the proletariat. They do not dare to socialise society against the bourgeoisie, they are afraid to rule without the old bureaucracy. The rule of the workers appears to them – even as to the bourgeoisie – to be chaos; their own theoretic inability makes them fear the gigantic task which the historical situation imposes upon the German proletariat. For this reason they want a National Constituent Assembly at the earliest possible moment to relieve them of responsibility.

The middle class also wants the convocation of this assembly because through it they hope to restore normal conditions, the establishment of a "stable" government which would send the councils home with expressions of thanks for services rendered. This has made some of the workers reflect and especially among the Independents they begin to doubt and strive to delay the convocation of the assembly. The Independents occupy in the coalition the place which the social-patriots formerly occupied in the bourgeois government, namely to prevent the workers from rebelling against the government. But they are compelled on account of the revolutionary tendencies amongst the workers, to resist the ultra-conservative dealings of the government.

This explains the growing friction between Kurt Eisner [since assassinated], the leader of the Bavarian Councils, and Barth, on one side, and Ebert and Scheidemann on the other. The Independents also propose plans for moderate socialisation – not all at once, no experiments! They propose beautiful plans for the upbuilding of Socialist production upon the basis of great industries and great agriculture whose support they must have. They do not think about the fact that Socialism is not a question of the nationalisation of industry, but is a question of the power of the proletariat – in the theoretic writings of Kautsky nothing is said about this! The result will be that when the bourgeoisie again assume power it will make an end of all these plans or realise them in its own way as State Socialism.

Besides the Independents already go arm in arm with Jaffe, the Bavarian Professor of Economy, who during the war outlined a project for extensive State Socialism, which is better called State Capitalism. The two parties, the majority Socialists and the Independents will, without a doubt, unite with the radical bourgeois parties upon this State Socialist programme, provided the proletariat does not intervene. While the Government is only concerned with externals and the maintenance of order – which, in reality, becomes increasingly chaotic – the friction between the classes develops. The bourgeoisie organise White Guards, the proletariat form Red Guards, and in secret reaction conspires and prepares for civil war. And while the arrival of troops strengthens the reactionaries, the revolutionary spirit flames amongst the workers.

The great struggle which must develop will be between the bourgeoisie, openly or covertly represented by the Social Democratic and the Independent parties, and the revolutionary movement, now called the Communist Party but which during the war was embodied in the Spartacus Group and the Bremen Internationalists. Although, as an organisation, it is not yet distinct and apart from the Social Democracy and the Independents the Communist Party is in direct opposition, it defends the dictatorship of the proletariat as against democratic parliamentarism and is opposed to the convocation of the National Assembly; it demands the abolition of Capitalism and the annulment of state debts. It represents the ideal of the Russian Bolshevik party although not directly connected with it, on account of friction between Rosa Luxemburg and Lenin. By the bourgeoisie and the Social Democracies the Communists are represented as being the Bolsheviki, and all the denunciation and misrepresentation directed against the Russian Bolsheviki are also directed against them. Many motions adopted by Soldiers' Councils – especially at the front, where they are least developed politically, and where, above all, they desire rest and peace – express their abhorrence of Bolshevism. As yet, the Communists are but a small minority, and the social-patriots and the bourgeoisie use this fact to consolidate their forces. The influence of the Communists upon the workers, however, is growing by leaps and bounds.

The international situation, the threatening food shortage and the menace of the Entente troops are great obstacles to revolutionary developments in Germany. From a military point of view Germany is absolutely at the mercy of the Entente, and, economically, she is also dependent upon the Allies. Her stores of foodstuffs are very small, and she is dependent upon the goodwill of the Poles for grain from the Eastern provinces. Through the loss of Lorraine Germany has not enough iron ore to supply her industries. The Entente had already notified her that the delivery of grain depends upon the maintenance of order and the establishment of an orderly government. The Entente, which sent troops to suppress Communistic Russia and restore the bourgeoisie, is careful not to allow a revolutionary Germany to assist Russia, even morally; and *Vorwaerts* – ever the lackey of the powers that be, first of Wilhelm, now of the Entente – is terribly agitated against the proposal of Russia to send representatives to the German Congress of Workers' and Soldiers' Councils. *Vorwaerts*, the bourgeois press, and the Government all combine to inspire the population with fear of the Entente threat, and to paint the economic situation as black as possible. They thus hope to stifle the revolutionary will of the workers, and it is beyond doubt that they will be successful with a considerable section of the masses.

There is little doubt but that the Congress of Workers' and Soldiers' Councils called for December 16th will support, by a big majority, the bourgeois government of Ebert-Haase. These councils are not by any means pure proletarian institutions; in the Soldiers' Councils are the officers; in the Workers' Councils are the Trade Union and party leaders. These men will not allow the revolution to go any further if they can prevent it.

But there are other objective material factors that will force the workers from the bottom up. In the first place the opposition between capital and labour – the first assault brought the proclamation of the eight-hour day and the establishment of the Workers' Councils in the factories. Now that the reaction is setting in the manufacturers are endeavouring to take back these concessions and reduce wages, while on the other hand, workers are demanding further reforms. Here and there clashes, in the shape of strikes, are occurring which require extraordinary efforts on the part of the Independent agents of the Government to conciliate. This will eventually compel the Government to act and force it to choose between pressing the bourgeoisie or having further sections of the masses arrayed against it. In the second place the economic want will effect the Government still more. The misery and deprivation the war has brought has been so horrible that the workers will not be able to carry any further burden, and if the Government does not actively assist them – and this means that it must take from the possessors – then the revolutionary spirit will receive fresh impetus among the masses.

In times of want, such as confront Germany now and in the coming years, only a government which by its deeds and its viewpoint will not be opposed to the great masses can exist. Consequently it is not to be expected that the present Government of Germany will be successful in confining the revolution to its present purely political reform character; but the attitude of the masses now in assisting the Government to a great extent, and is, therefore, strengthening the bourgeoisie, and will increase its power of resistance in the coming civil war.

Much depends on the class instincts of the coming Congress of Workers' and Soldiers' Councils. If it will lay the foundation for power, the power of the workers and soldiers, then the proletariat will be well armed for the coming struggle.

Anton Pannekoek, of the Communist Party of Holland

PART THREE
Sylvia Pankhurst

Communism and its Tactics

Part One
Workers Dreadnought , November 26th, 1921

Under Communism all shall satisfy their material needs without stint or measure from the common storehouse, according to their desires. Everyone will be able to have what he or she desires in food, in clothing, books, music, education and travel facilities. The abundant production now possible, and which invention will constantly facilitate, will remove any need for rationing or limiting of consumption.

Every individual, relying on the great common production, will be secure from material want and anxiety.

There will be no class distinctions, since these arise from differences in material possessions, education and social status — all such distinctions will be swept away.

There will be neither rich nor poor. Money will no longer exist, and none will desire to hoard commodities not in use, since a fresh supply may be obtained at will. There will be no selling, because there will be no buyers, since everyone will be able to obtain everything at will, without payment.

The possession of private property, beyond that which is in actual personal use, will disappear.

There will be neither masters nor servants, all being in a position of economic equality — no individual will be able to become the employer of another.

All children will be educated up to adult age, and all adults will be able to make free, unstinted use of all educational facilities in their abundant leisure.

Stealing, forgery, burglary, and all economic crimes will disappear, with all the objectionable apparatus for preventing, detecting and punishing them.

Prostitution will become extinct; it is a commercial transaction, dependent upon the economic need of the prostitute and the customer's power to pay.

Sexual union will no longer be based upon material conditions, but will be freely contracted on the basis of affection and mutual attraction.

The birth of children will cease to be prevented by reason of poverty.

Material anxiety being removed, and the race for wealth eliminated, other objects and ambitions will take the place of the personal struggle for individual material existence; since all will benefit from the labour of all honour will be done, not to the wealthy, as at present, but to those who are skilful and zealous in the common service.

Emulation in work will take the place of emulation in wealth.

With the disappearance of the anxious struggle for existence, which saps the energy and cripples initiative, a new vigour, a new independence will develop. People will have more courage to desire freedom, greater determination to possess it. They will be more exacting in their demands upon life, more fastidious as to their choice of a vocation. They will wish to work at what they enjoy, to order their lives as they desire. Work will be generally enjoyed as never before in the history of mankind.

The desire for freedom will be tempered by the sense of responsibility towards the commonweal, which will provide security for all.

Public opinion provides a stronger, more general compulsion than any penal code, and public opinion will strongly disapprove idleness and waste.

To secure the abundant production necessary to Communism, and to cope with the ever-growing complexity of modern life and requirements, large-scale production and co-operative effort is necessary. The people of today would not be willing to go back to producing everything by hand in domestic workshops; were they to do so, they could not maintain the population in comfort and with reasonable leisure. The people of today would be unwilling to abandon all the productive factories, the trains, the electric generating stations and so on. The retention of such things necessitates the working-together of large numbers of people. As soon as numbers of people are working together and supplying with their products numbers of other people, some sort of organisation of work and of distribution becomes inevitable. The work itself cannot be carried on without organisation. In each industry, either the workers concerned in the work must form and control the organisation, or they will be under the dominion of the organisers. The various industries are interlocked in interest and utility; therefore the industrial organisations must be interlocked.

When wages have disappeared, when all are upon a basis of economic equality, when the position of manager, director, organiser, etc., brings no material advantage, the desire for it will be less widespread and less keen, and the danger of oppressive action by the management will be largely nullified. Nevertheless, management imposed on unwilling subordinates will not be tolerated; where the organiser has chosen the assistants, the assistants will be free to leave, or change him; where the assistants choose the organiser, they will be free to change him. Co-operation for the common good is necessary, but freedom, not domination, is the goal.

Since co-operative work and mutual reliance on mutual aid renders some kind of organisation necessary, the best possible form of organisation must be chosen: the test of its worth is its efficiency and the scope for freedom and initiative it allows to each of its units.

The Soviet structure of committees and delegates, built up from the base of the workshop and village assembly, presents the best form of organisation yet evolved; it arises naturally when the workers are thrown upon their own resources in the matter of government.

The Soviet structure will undoubtedly be the organisational structure of Communism, at any rate for some time to come. We live always, however, in a state of flux, and there is and happily can be, no permanence about human institutions; there is always the possibility of something higher, as yet undiscovered.

The overthrow of Capitalism precedent to the establishment of Communism will be resisted by the possessors of wealth. Thus Capitalism will only be overthrown by revolution.

The revolution can only come when conditions are ripe for it; but opportunities may be missed: the rising may fail to take place at the opportune moment, or it may fail by mismanagement of the proletarian forces. A partial success may be achieved, and if Capitalism is not completely destroyed, it may afterwards re-establish itself, as it speedily did in Hungary, as it is gradually doing in Russia.

Part Two
Workers Dreadnought, December 3rd 1921

Since the overthrow of capitalism would be resisted by the possessors of wealth, whether this were effected by Act of Parliament or by a sudden revolt of the people, it is absolutely necessary for the Communists to prepare the working class for such resistance. Many people still doubt that capitalist resistance to the overthrow of capitalism will go to the length of civil war, yet there is abundant contemporary evidence to prove that such resistance will be made.

Here in Britain we have the Ulster capitalists' preparations for armed resistance to the Asquith Home Rule Act. The civil war threats and preparations by Ulster Capitalism were and are supported by British Toryism. That is why it succeeds. Since British and Ulster landlords and capitalists have thought it worthwhile to resort to the extreme of civil war on the Irish question how absolutely certain it is that they would do so to prevent the establishment of Communism and proletarian rule!

In Finland, in Central Europe, in Russia, the same thing has been seen; when capitalism is in danger capitalism resorts to force of arms to protect itself. In Italy too, the fascisti, with their armed attacks on Communists, Socialists, Trade Unionists, and Co-operators; attacks organised by the Capitalists who use these disorderly bands as their tools, are but another evidence of the same fact: when the established order is in danger its beneficiaries arm to protect it; its supporters and opponents come to blows, civil war breaks out and for the time being peace is no more.

Is that as it should be? It is as it is. The inevitable must be recognised and prepared for. A determined struggle for supremacy inevitably accompanies the overthrow of capitalism.

Experience shows that the crisis arises suddenly: the old relationship has been growing more and more strained, and suddenly the bonds are snapped and the storm bursts. We do not say that a Parliamentary crisis could not be the last straw that would precipitate the revolution, but in none of the contemporary revolutions has this been so. We have now the experience of Russia, Finland, Germany (where there have been a revolution and several attempts at further revolution), in Austria and Hungary to look to.

Great economic pressure, fired by a great rebellion against the actions and ideology of those who have been in power, is the factor which produces the proletarian revolution. Parliament must be overthrown with the capitalist system if the proletarian revolution is to succeed there must be a clean break with the old institutions of Government; the revolution must create its own instrument.

Parliament would have to be sacrificed with the overthrow of capitalism, even were it conceivable that an Act of Parliament will formally abolish the capitalist system. The capitalists would resist by force the first attempt to put the Act into practice, and Parliament is not the body that could carry the proletarian revolution through to success in face of capitalist revolt, which would be one of both armed and passive resistance.

The workers would be compelled to meet such a revolt with all the forces at their disposal; their most characteristic weapon is their industrial power, for the effective wielding of which they would have to be co-ordinated industrially. Every industry would be divided against itself; the owners and part of the management would take the capitalist side, the mass of the workers the side of the working class. As in all the countries where the revolutionary crisis has appeared, the naval and military forces would be divided in the same way, though the old training and discipline would probably cause a larger proportion of the working class rank-and-file to support the side of the master class than would be the case in industry.

A little consideration of such a situation must reveal to anyone who thinks seriously that Parliament and the local governing bodies; the county and borough councils, the boards of guardians, and so on, could not be the guiding and co-ordinating machinery of such a struggle; that such machinery could take no other form than that of the Soviets.

Even in a war between rival capitalist governments Parliament becomes a cipher in the struggle; the machinery that carries out the war is the Cabinet composed of the heads of the various Departments of State, all very much controlled by the expert managers of those departments. On the military side the political and military heads of the War Office work in contact with a machine which is composed of all the officers from the highest to the lowest in the army, and the men under their command. On the industrial side the political and technical heads of the departments work through a machine which is composed of the owners, managers and workers in all industries, factories, workshops.

So it will be in the proletarian revolution, but this being a struggle between the workers and their masters, the officers and the managers will be proletarian leaders chosen by their fellows. And contact with the rank and file will be by delegates and mass meetings. The services of the rank and file will not be based on compulsion and wagery, but on consent and enthusiasm and a voice in responsibility for aims and policies.

War experience will show us that even capitalism found that shop stewards and councils on which Trade Union officials co-operated with the management were helpful in securing greater output, which was necessary to their success in war.

Some people may say that the Soviets could be abandoned and Parliament reverted to after the clash of civil war had passed; and that, as they hope there may be no such clash, they will not interest themselves in the question of Soviets. Further consideration should show them, however, that even were hope of avoiding a struggle with capitalism justified, Parliament would have to go and the Soviets would become necessary at least for some time after the overthrow of capitalism.

Consider the position here in London with capitalism abolished; the tubes, trams and buses, the main line stations, the docks, the reservoirs, the gas works, the electric generating stations, the bakeries, food preserving, clothing and other factories, the slaughter-houses, butchers, bakers, greengrocers, grocers and other wholesale and retail shops and the markets. Millions of people are waiting for their daily supply of milk and bread to be brought round to them, to find their daily supply of provender in the shops where they deal, their habitual means of transport. If any of these things stop, then at least some people will not arrive at their daily work, and masses of others may thus be deprived of accustomed necessaries. Perhaps the workers are already engaged in a general strike; perhaps the wheels of industry and transport are already dislocated, and everyone is already living a hungry, makeshift existence.

Whichever way it be, everything has to be reorganised and built up on a new basis; production for use, not for profit, and capitalism is overthrown. Undoubtedly some of those who used to manage the big concerns under the old system have refused to function any more; undoubtedly many others can not be trusted to occupy such important positions of trust; already they have shown their hostility and have taken to sabotage. And there are the people, the hungering millions of all sorts, clamouring to have their wants supplied, each with their peculiarities, their likes and dislikes, their reasonable and unreasonable prejudices, and crowds of them ready to start looting if they are kept waiting or denied what they are accustomed to have and what they think is their due. Everyone, both as worker and consumer, has new hopes and desires and new claims upon life, for has not the Workers' Revolution come? Everyone demands more leisure and more congenial labour, more food, more clothes, more pleasure; only the patient people are prepared to wait, and everyone is finding his daily work, assuming he is prepared to do it as of old, quite dislocated. Everyone, too, is demanding a new independent status, and a share in deciding how things shall be done.

Imagine bringing unfortunate Parliament into such a dilemma. Frank Hodges and T.C. Cramp besieged by a mob of Westminster housewives who cannot obtain either fish or butter. Will Thorne, who is told the electricity supply is cut off in all the suburbs. Ramsay Macdonald, some of whose constituents are tramping to London to tell him that Leicester can get no coal.

The only chance for that Parliament would be to call the Industrial Soviets into being!

As to the borough councils: we remember the little matter of the food rationing, and the groups of housewives here and there who, through the muddles of the local food committee and the Ministry of Food, found themselves as "outlanders" prohibited from buying at the shops where they had hitherto dealt, and unable to procure commodities anywhere else.

The only people who could deal with the great new situation would be the people who do the work and the people who use the produce. All interlocked as they are in this busy hive of overcrowded life the Soviets would be the only solution. The workers in the factory in a turmoil of dislocation would come together and talk the matter over; appoint one of their number to answer the telephone, another to fetch supplies; others to take stock; others, according to their capacities, to mind the various machines, others to acquaint the absentees that the factory is at work again, others as organisers and instructors. They would send to the workers in other factories for more supplies and organise exchanges.

The women rushing frantically about in search of supplies, and threatening to start looting and rioting because their children are hungry, would be called together by the more level-headed, would enumerate their wants and place their demands before the workers responsible for production and transport.

Part Three
Workers Dreadnought December 10 1921

In Russia all this was done, and over vast districts, under the spur of need without preliminary thought or organisation.

In this country the workers cannot leave things to chance. Capitalism is highly organised here and will defeat the workers' revolution again and again, unless the workers are organised efficiently. Moreover, in London and in the vast chains of towns which form our industrial districts we are so closely massed on the ground, so absolutely dependent on food brought in from outside, and upon the collective service of the whole industrial community, that unless production and distribution is well organised we must speedily starve.

It will go hard with us if we have not created the machinery before the hour of revolution strikes.

The machinery of the Soviets must obviously follow, and does so far as it is successful, the lines of need. Each workshop has its meetings and elects its delegates to a factory committee. The factory will also have its mass meetings of all workers on occasion. Every factory will be united to the factories of the same industry in the district through its committee of delegates, and in the same way will be co-ordinated with every factory in the same industry in the country. These are the bodies which will meet and discuss what concerns the industry, but for matters which concern the district in which the workers live and work they will go to mass meetings or send delegates to committees from all the industries in the district. The housekeepers will have their own meetings also, and they, too, will go to mass meetings or send delegates to the producing industries when arrangements are to be made between them.

All this will be done purely by way of managing affairs so that all may be, as far as possible, satisfied that the needs of all may be explained and understood by those who have to supply them.

But there should be no compulsion; some people may say: "What the majority decide is good enough for me." Others will say: "I like to have a voice in it." As a rule, when things affecting a group of people who are working together come up for decision everyone of the group will join in and give his or her opinion, and generally the thing will be decided by mutual agreement.

The Dictatorship of the Proletariat

The dictatorship of the proletariat is a much misused phrase; when Communism is in being there will be no proletariat, as we understand the term today, and no dictatorship.

The dictatorship, so far as it is genuine and defensible, is the suppression by Workers' Soviets of capitalism and the attempt to re-establish it. This should be a temporary state of war. Such a period will inevitably occur, we believe, because we do not believe that the possessors of wealth will submit to the overthrow of capitalism without resistance. On the contrary, we believe the owners will fight to preserve capitalism by every means in their power.

Whilst the capitalists are openly fighting the workers who have seized the power, fighting them openly and secretly in armed battalions in guerilla bands, by ambush, assassination, bombs, sabotage, spies; then the proletariat must maintain a vigilant war service and dictatorship. The situation in Ireland before the truce is a little like what a proletarian dictatorship may have to cope with.

Once, however, the war is over, once the capitalist and his allies have given up any serious attempt to re-establish capitalism, then away with dictatorship; away with compulsion.

Compulsion of any kind is repugnant to the Communist ideal. No-one may make a wage-slave of another; no-one may hoard up goods for himself that he does not require and cannot use; but the only way to prevent such practices is not by making them punishable; it is by creating a society in which no-one needs to become a wage slave, and no-one cares to be cumbered with a private hoard of goods when all that he needs is readily supplied as he needs it from the common storehouse.

Compulsory education for children has been a protection for children in this capitalist society when parents are poor and grasping enough to desire the earnings of their children or to suffer from the burden of their maintenance, but when all things that nature and mankind produce are free in abundance for the asking what parents would deny education to their children; what children would submit with the school-door freely open?

Part Four
Workers Dreadnought, December 24th 1921 and January 21st 1922

We have seen that the Soviets are destined both to provide the organisational machinery of Communist society and to act as the instrument of the proletarian dictatorship during the transitional period in which, whilst capitalism has been overthrown, the dispossessed owners have not yet settled down to accept the new order. The Soviets may also conduct the fight for the actual overthrow of Capitalism, though in Russia the power was actually seized by the Bolshevik Party; then handed to the Soviets.

Let us consider the essential structure of the Soviet, its particular characteristic, wherein lies its special fitness to function as the administrative machinery of the Communist community.

The Soviet is constructed along the lines of production and distribution; it replaces not merely Parliament and the present local governing bodies, but also the capitalists, managerial staffs and employees of today with all their ramifications. The functional units of the Soviets are the groups of workers of all grades, including those engaged in management in the factory, the dockyard, the mine, the farm, the warehouse, the office, the distributive store, the school, the hospital, the printing shop, the laundry, the restaurant, and the domestic workers in the communal household, the street or block of dwellings.

The generally accepted theoretical structure of the Soviet community is as follows:

Industrial Co-ordination

The Workshop Committee: comprising all the workers in the shop.

The Factory Committee: comprising delegates from the Workshop Committees.

The District Committee: comprising delegates from the factory or sub-district committees of the workers in the industry, and from district committees of distributive workers engaged in distributing the products of the industry.

The National Committee: composed of delegates from district committees.

Inter-industrial Co-ordination

District and Sub-District Committees: Delegates from district or sub district committees of industries (including factories, docks, farms, laundries, restaurants, centres of distribution, schools, domestic workers, parks, theatres, etc., workers in all branches of social activity being represented).

National Committee: comprising delegates of district committees of all industries and works of social activity.

Thus there is a dual machinery: 1. For the organisation and co-ordination of each industry and social activity; 2. for the linking together of all industries and social activities.

The network of committees of delegates which makes up the framework of the Soviets and links the many productive groups, and also individual producers should not be regarded as a rigid, cast-iron machinery, but as a convenient means of transacting necessary business, a practical method of inter-organisation which gives everyone the opportunity of a voice in social management. The members of a community are dependent upon each other. The cotton spinning mill is operated by a number of groups of workers practising various crafts. The workers in the spinning mill are dependent for the execution of their work on the cotton growers, the railwaymen, the mariners, and the dockers, who provide them with the raw material of their trade. They are dependent on machine makers, miners, electricians and others for the machinery of spinning and the power to run it, and on the weaver, the bleacher, the dyer, the printer, the garment worker and upholsterer to complete the work they have begun. In order that the spinners may do their work they are also dependent on builders, decorators, furniture makers, food producers, garment makers, and innumerable others whose labours are necessary to maintain them in health and efficiency.

At present it is the employer who directs, the merchant who co-ordinates and distributes social production. When capitalism is destroyed another medium of direction, co-ordination and distribution must be discovered, the productive processes must not fall into chaos. The Soviets will supply the necessary medium of co-ordination and direction; but they must become a medium of convenience, not of compulsion; otherwise there can be no genuine Communism.

In Russia the Soviet constitution has only been very partially applied, and has not been theoretically regular in structure, and is still constantly subject to large modifications.

The Russian Soviets had not been created in advance in preparation for the revolution of March, 1917: they sprang into life in the time of crisis. They had arisen in the revolution of 1905, but had died away at its fall. The March, 1917, revolution only created Soviets in a few centres, and though their number grew and was added to by the November Bolshevik revolution, even yet the network of Soviets is incomplete. Kameneff, reporting on this question to the seventh all-Russian Congress of Soviets in 1920, stated that even where Soviets existed their general assemblies were often rare, and when held frequently only listened to a few speeches and dispersed without transacting any real business.

Nevertheless, the Soviet government had claimed that the number of Soviets actually functioning has grown continuously; yet it freely admits that the Soviets have taken neither so active nor so responsible a part as they should in the creation and management of the new community. Russia's "new economic policy" of reversion to capitalism strikes at the root of the Soviet idea and destroys the functional status of the Soviets.

Russia's special difficulties in applying the Soviet system were inherent in the backward state of the country which had only partially progressed from feudalism into capitalism. In industry the small home producer still accounted for 60 per cent of Russia's industrial production. In agriculture the peasants had not yet been divorced from the land as is the case in England, where we have long had a completely landless class of rural workers. In Russia the ideal of the land worker was to produce for himself on his own holding and to sell his products, not to work in co-operation with others. The Russian peasants, vastly outnumbering the rest of the population, were all but unanimous in their demands. Those who had no land were determined to get a piece for themselves, and those who had a little piece of land wanted more. Though their individualism was tempered by the old custom of periodically re-dividing the land and other village traditions, the peasants were an influence against Communism. Nevertheless, their ancient village council, the Mir, a survival from the period of primitive Communism, had somewhat prepared them for the Soviets.

In the scattered village communities the occupational character of the Soviet is apparently somewhat submerged in the territorial; yet all the subsidiary crafts of the villages are attendant on the great industry of agriculture. Ties of common interest and mutual dependence, which are the life-blood of the Soviet, are clearly apparent between the land workers and the various craftsmen of the village. The blurring of the occupational character of the village Soviet does not detract from its function of an administrative unit in harmony with the actual conditions of the country. On the other hand, the fact that the town Soviets could not supply it with the industrial products it needed, by weakening the link of mutual usefulness, making the usefulness merely one-sided, removed the natural impetus of the Soviets of the villages to link themselves for utilitarian reasons with the Soviets of the towns. Production by individual producers who are competing with each other creates sources of conflict which are antagonistic to the Soviet. The strongest and most useful Soviet must always be that which is formed of those who are working together and who realise at every turn that they are dependent on each other. The necessity for the Soviet becomes more pronounced and its work more varied the more that work is carried on in common and the more closely the lives of the people are related to each other. Mankind is gregarious; the degree of gregariousness in human beings is partly dependant on material conditions, partly on inclination (which is doubtless largely, if not wholly, the slow product of long environment). As humanity secures a completer mastery over matter, individual choice as to how life shall be spent, becomes broader and more free; science will more and more enable desire to determine the degree of industrial concentration. Our civilisation has perhaps nearly reached the limit of the tendency to gather together ever greater and greater numbers of workers, performing some tiny mechanical operation as attendants to machinery. Perhaps the future has in store for us an entirely opposite development. That would not effect the fact that the Soviet must find its most congenial soil in a society based on mutual aid and mutual dependence.

In the industrial centres where it might have been expected that the occupational basis of the Soviet would have been adhered to, the structure of the Russian Soviets was irregular from the theoretical standpoint. The Soviets, instead of being formed purely of workers in the various industries and activities of the community, were composed also of delegates of political parties, political groups formed by foreigners in Russia, Trades Councils, Trade Unions and co-operative societies. Pravda of April 18th, 1918, published the following regulations for the Moscow Soviet elections:

"Regulations for Representation.

"Establishments employing 200 to 500 workers, one representative; those employing over 500, send one representative for every 500 men. Establishments employing less than 200 workers, combine for purpose of representation with other small establishments.

"Ward Soviets send two deputies, elected at a plenary session.

"Trade Unions with a membership not exceeding 2,000, send one deputy; not exceeding 5,000, two deputies; above 5,000, one for every 5,000 workers, but not more than ten deputies for any one union.

"The Moscow Trades' Council sends five deputies. "Political parties send 30 deputies to the Soviet: the seats are allotted to the parties in proportion to their membership, providing the parties include four representatives of industrial establishments and organised workers.

"Representatives of the following National non-Russian Socialist parties, one representative per party, are allotted seats: —

(a) "Bund" (Jewish).
(b) Polish Socialist Party (Left).
(c) Polish and Lithuanian Social Democratic Parties.
(d) Lettish Social Democratic Party.
(e) Jewish Social Democratic Party."

The intention in giving representation to these various interests was, of course, to disarm their antagonism to the Soviet power and to secure their co-operation instead; but the essential administrative character of the Soviets was thereby sacrificed. Constituted thus they must inevitably discuss political antagonisms rather than the production and distribution of social utilities and amenities.

The industrial unions, economic councils and co-operative societies which have been a feature of Soviet Russia (the two former having representation in the Soviets) have no place, because they have no reason for existence, under an efficient Soviet system, in which they would be absorbed into the occupational Soviets and indistinguishably fused with them.

Industrial unions can have no reason for existence if the Soviets are fulfilling efficiently their proper function as the administrative machinery of the Communist community, for the Soviets should cover the same constituencies as the industrial unions. The industrial unions will only exist so long as there is either a conflict between the workers and the Soviets (which are theoretically the organs of the workers), or in case the Soviets are failing to administer industry or administer it efficiently. The very existence of the Industrial Union, unless it be merely a social club, denotes an antagonism between the members of the union and those who are administering industry; unless, on the other hand, the Soviets are failing to administer industry and the unions are formed for that purpose. In Russia, as a matter of fact, the continued existence of the industrial unions is due to the fact that there it antagonism between the workers and those who are administering industry. In a theoretically correct Soviet community the workers, through their Soviets, which are indistinguishable from them, should administer. This has not been achieved in Russia.

Co-operatives have no place in a genuine Soviet community. If they are distributive organisations purely, they should be the distributive branches of the industrial Soviets. If they are organs of buying and selling, they are survivals of capitalism and must disappear under Communism. If they are associations of producers they can only differ from industrial Soviets in so far as they exact payment in cash or kind for their produce instead of distributing it freely. In so far as they exact payment or practice barter, they have no place in a Soviet community.

The curious overlapping patchwork which has hitherto made up the Russian Soviet system should by no means be slavishly copied. The Russians themselves have emphasised that. Nevertheless, the recent tactics which they have induced the Third International to adopt do not indicate that they have a clear perception that a highly organised industrial community may build the new Communist order on the theoretically correct foundation of the occupational Soviets.

Part Five
Workers Dreadnought January 28th 1922

Zinoviev, at the Second Congress of the Third International in Moscow, introduced a Thesis declaring that no attempt should be made to form Soviets prior to the outbreak of the revolutionary crisis. It was argued that, as such bodies would be powerless, or nearly so, their formation might bring the conception of the Soviets into proletarian contempt. The Thesis was adopted by the Congress, without discussion, and thereby became an axiom of the Third International.

The question as to whether the mere borrowed term, Soviet, shall be reserved for use in the actual crisis of revolution is of small importance though, if not used previously, it would probably miss being adopted as the slogan of the revolution.

The question of postponing the creation of the actual organisation till the hour of a revolutionary crisis is, on the other hand, a fundamental one.

The idea expressed and insisted upon in that Thesis of Zinoviev's was that the Soviet must be a great mass movement, coming together in the electrical excitement of the crisis; the correctness of its structure, its actual Sovietness (to coin an adjective), being considered of secondary importance. A progressive growth, gradually branching out till the hour of crisis; a strong and well-tried organisation is not contemplated by the Thesis. The need for carefully conceived structure is ignored. Propaganda for the Soviets alone is recommended.

Russia's dual Revolution was an affair of spontaneous outbursts, with no adequate organisation behind it. The Trade Unions, always a feeble growth, were crushed by the Czardom at the outbreak of the great war of 1914. The Revolutionary political parties could call for a revolution; they could not carry it through: that was accomplished by the action of the revolutionary elements in the Army and Navy, in the workshops, on the railways, and on the land. That these revolutionaries at the point of production were mainly unorganised was a disability, not an advantage. In Russia the government first of the Czar, then of Kerensky, crumbled readily under the popular assault. The disability arising from the disorganised state of the workers was not felt in its full weightiness until after the Soviet Government had been established. Then it was realised that, though the Soviets were supposed to have taken power, the Soviet structure had yet to be created and made to function. The structure is still incomplete: it has functioned hardly at all. Administration has been largely by Government departments, working often without the active, ready co-operation, sometimes even with the hostility of groups of workers who ought to have been taking a responsible share in administration. To this cause must largely be attributed Soviet Russia's defeat on the economic front.

It would be monstrous folly for workers in other countries, especially in highly industrialised countries where Capitalism is old, to imitate Russia's unpreparedness. We in Britain have an infinitely stronger Capitalism to overturn: we have greater opportunities of creating the organisation necessary to fight it.

This organisation must be able both to attack and destroy Capitalism in the final struggle, and also to replace the administrative machinery of Capitalism. Moreover it must be animated by the will to these achievements.

We have at present no such organisation in this country.

Our Trade Unions have neither the will, nor the capacity for the purpose. We are nearest industrial unionism in mining and transport and on the land, but even there we have several competing Unions in each industry. In the textile, metal, food preparing, woodworking, clothing, and building industries, we have a multiplicity of little-co-ordinated organisations. Moreover, the great mass of the workers is divided into two sections: the skilled and the unskilled: organised into quite separate Unions and divided by impassable barriers which have been jealously erected and maintained by the skilled workers.

The structure of the Trade Unions is antiquated and fruitful of delays. It is highly undemocratic, some Unions have first and second class members, the former, of ten or more years' standing, alone being eligible for office; some elect their executive for eight years or some other long term; some hold no general congress of branch representatives. The rank and file members of the Unions have little or no voice in deciding the larger issues of policy. The executive usually determining the policy to be pursued at national conferences with other bodies. The rules, which are registered with the capitalist Government's Registrar General, cannot be changed without long and hard effort. Under normal circumstances it must take many years to change them appreciably. The rules and structure of the Unions would place a handicap upon any serious attempt that might be made to remould the Unions in order that they might function with some sort of efficiency in the attack on Capitalism and in the administration of industry after Capitalism were overthrown.

The rules and structure are even a serious handicap in the daily struggle to palliate Capitalism, which is what the Unions exist for.

The Union officials who, almost to a man, desire the retention of the capitalist system, fear, above all things, any serious attack upon it, are aided and protected in their conservatism by the Union rules.

The reactionary officials have, however, a stronger buttress and protection in the backward masses, who vastly outnumber the awakened workers in the Trade Unions. It is only in the advanced stages of the Revolution that the great masses will discern the gulf between themselves and their reactionary leaders. This is one of the reasons why another organisation is necessary. Such an organisation must reveal to the masses the true character of their leaders, and offer them an alternative policy.

The Trade Unions are composed of masses of workers who did not become members of the Unions with the object of changing the social system, but merely to palliate it. Latterly men and women have even been forced into the Unions, because Trade Unions had become strong enough to insure that those who refused to join would have difficulty in obtaining employment. With such a membership, the Trade Unions are naturally timid, conservative bodies, apt to oppose drastic change and unready to take any bold initiative.

We believe that such Trade Unions can never deliberately precipitate a revolution. In this matter, theory is supported by experience. In Russia the revolution was not made by the hardly-existing Trade Unions. After the first revolution the Central Council of Soviets laboured to form Trade Unions. Some of the Unions it had formed then opposed retention of power by the Soviets, worked against all tendencies towards Communism, and gave their support to the demand for a bourgeois republic, with Capitalism re-established in power.

In Germany, the Trade Unions, so far from leading the various proletarian uprisings, took no official part except to oppose them.

To administer in place of Capitalism, as well as to overthrow it, the workers should be organised with all, and more than all, the efficiency and coherence of Capitalism. In this country, Capitalism itself, though tremendously better equipped than in Russia under the Czardom, still lacks co-ordination. As a medium for supplying the people's needs, it suffers on the one hand from the competition and overlapping of private interests; and, on the other, from shortage and lack in districts where the small means of the people do not render it profitable to supply them efficiently. Every day British Capitalism is remedying some of its organisational defects, at least, some of those due to its own internal capitalist rivalries.

From banking, where we have nearly arrived at a single trust, to tea-shops, where Lyons is absorbing competitor after competitor, co-ordination and the elimination of competition is going on constantly. Trustification has not yet developed nearly so far in Britain as in Germany, where the combination of the powerful capitalist, Stinnes, links up coal and ore mining, smelting, and the manufacture, shipping and marketing of all sorts of metal goods; forestry, wood-working, paper-making, printing and publishing; tram, train, and sea travel, and the provision of hotel accommodation; the production and supply of electricity in all its branches, and a host of other activities.

British Capitalist organisation will rapidly become more closely knit under pressure of the competition which is rising up against it all over the world: in Britain's own colonies and dominions, in America, in the growing industrialism of Poland, Italy, and other European countries, above all in Germany, whose Capitalism, still more since the war that was meant to crush it, is Britain's keenest rival.

We should welcome the trustification of industry, in so far as it is a co-ordination along the lines of convenience and utility in producing and distributing what is needed by the populace. We should welcome it also because it provides the means of linking up the workers into a closely-knit fighting organisation; an organisation which can step in and displace the capitalist, and, having done so, shall be able to carry on production and distribution.

Such an organisation may be built up by organising the workers in the co-ordinated centres of production and distribution along the lines of the Trust itself. The Trade Unions are not thus organised.

Although Trustification has not yet developed very far in Britain, British employers of labour are much better organised than British workers. Employers' Associations and Trade Journals bind the employers together in all industries, and a much greater degree of solidarity is shown by the employing class than by the working class when a trade dispute arises. In this country Trade Unionism has never achieved the general strike: it has even shrunk from attempting any large-scale sympathetic strike. In this respect British Trade Unionism is behind that of most European countries. Both ideologically and structurally it is distinctly outdistanced by its continental contemporaries. Indeed, it is solely on the size of its membership that the British Trade Union movement has claimed to be the strongest in the world. As a body of action it would gain in strength if it could be ruthlessly pruned of its more backward members.

The trustification and co-ordination of industry under Capitalism has for many years been causing a perpetual discussion upon industrial unionism to be carried on in the Labour movement; but the result in actual improvements in the Union structure has been surprisingly small.

That rapid wartime growth, the Shop Stewards' organisation, in a few months co-ordinated the workers in the munition factories and shipyards with an efficient completeness the Trade Unions had never approached, and made the Stewards' movement a coherent acting force, such as the Trade Unions had never been. This development shows that the task of organising the workers in accordance with Capitalist organisation, in which the Trade Unions have hitherto failed, may readily be accomplished by building upon a new basis, unhindered by the trammels of the old machinery and the prejudices and vested interests of the old officials.

It may, perhaps, be objected that since the Shop Stewards' organisation dwindled at the close of the war and has all but passed away, there are elements of permanency in the Trade Unions which the Shop Stewards did not possess. That is true. The Trade Unions remained in possession of their accumulated funds, and were adding to these funds week by week, for the workers continued paying their Trade Union dues week by week; although the Trade Unions were functioning only as benefit societies, whilst the rank and file workers themselves were doing, through their shop committees and their elected stewards, the work for which the Unions were created. The Unions retained possession of the funds and the friendly benefits. When the boom in production passed and unemployment became rife in the land, the workers unready for the time being to safeguard their status in the workshop, were glad to fall back on the friendly benefits of the Union.

Part Six
Workers Dreadnought February 4th 1922

As we have seen, the main purpose of the Soviets is to minister to the needs of the people, in clothing, housing, education, recreation, transport and so on. The workers who are responsible for these services are linked together in their Soviets for the purposes of their work. The Soviet structure is efficient, because it is formed on the lines necessitated by the work; also because it gives every worker a responsible share in the common effort, and thereby encourages the co-operative impulse. Even under Capitalism the merits of the workshop council, which is the germ of the Soviet, have been discovered, not only by the workers, but by the capitalist himself. During the war, when the Shop Stewards' Movement flourished, employers actually initiated the formation of shop councils and the election of workers' stewards.

The employers did so, not merely to forestall the rebel elements, but rather because, in the great stress of war-time and with a tremendous influx of new workers, the shop council organisation would minimise the cost of management, reduce the number of paid supervisors required, and the difficulty of maintaining discipline, and increase the output by producing a spirit of willingness amongst the workers who were responsive to the patriotic appeals to produce more.

Mr. Charles Reynold, of the big engineering firm of that name, recently gave an address on workshop committees and the control of industry: he described how the works committee at his firm holds monthly meetings with the management to discuss wages and conditions of labour, and all questions of management. He declared that the confidential financial information presented to the directors is communicated to the works committee, and the result is the creation of a sense of responsibility, an understanding of the management point of view, and the acceptance of changes with comparatively little friction.

From the class-war standpoint this information does not gratify us, and presumably the scheme is part of some profit-sharing arrangement. It is nevertheless testimony to the value of the workshop council from the administrative efficiency standpoint, although under Capitalism the shop council has, of course, no real power, and only a leading-strings share of responsibility. Reynold's is but one of many capitalist firms which are endeavouring, in the interests of efficiency, to secure the co-operation of their workers, though capitalist conditions prevent the co-operation from being genuine on either side. The growth of Whitleyism shows that the intelligent British capitalists are beginning to understand that men and women only give their best when they give of their free will, feeling that they are responsible entities. This truth is too often forgotten by those who once preached it, when they attain to official positions, whether in Russia, or in Britain.

The trend of the times supports the view that the Soviet Government made a serious blunder when it decided (and put into practice its decision) that "workers' control of industry" is only a slogan useful for securing the overthrow of the capitalist, and must be discarded, once the workers have turned out the capitalist, in favour of management by an individual or committee appointed by some centralised authority.

A careful and candid survey of the Russian attempt to establish Communism will some day reveal, more clearly than at present, the proportional weight of the causes which have led to its failure. That it has failed for the present, and that only a powerful new impetus can stop the present retrogression in Russia we are compelled to admit.

Such a candid survey will provide evidence as to how far the Russian failure has been due to the capitalist resistance to Communism; how far to the unreadiness of the population; how far to the mistakes of the Communists, and especially to the mistakes of the Soviet Government.

The question of workers' control of industry will bulk largely in this connection.

Viewed from the standpoint of efficiency as a fighting force, it is notorious that never were strikes so swiftly, solidly and successfully effected in this country as those of the war-time Shop Stewards' movement. A rank and file chorus complaining of the inefficiency, inactivity and lack of class solidarity shown by the reactionary Trade Union leaders is constantly rising and falling. During the Dublin Lock-Out of 1912, during the railway strike of 1919 and the coal strike of 1921, it swelled with indignation, but only the workers organised in the workshop committees have taken large-scale action, except at the bidding of the Union officials. This is not unnatural: until both the individual workers and the workers in each individual firm feel that others will act with them, they shrink from taking action which, if not supported, will lead to their victimisation.

To recapitulate: the Soviets, or workers' occupational councils, will form the administrative machinery for supplying the needs of the people in Communist society; they will also make the revolution by seizing control of all the industries and services of the community.

Though in Russia the revolution was accomplished by Soviets which sprang up spontaneously in some places and by unorganised mob risings, this was only possible, because the government of Russia had broken down, Capitalism was weak and of limited extent, and the entire country in a state of chaotic disorder.

Here in Britain the machinery of the Soviets must be prepared in advance. In all the industries and services, revolutionary workers, who are habitually at work there and know the ropes, must be prepared to seize and maintain control.

The Trade Unions do not provide this machinery: they are not competent, either to seize, control, or to administer industry. They are not structurally fitted to administer industry, because their organisations do not combine all the workers in any industry, and they are not efficiently co-ordinated. Their branches are constructed according to the district in which the worker resides, not according to where he works.

The Trade Unions are, moreover opposed to revolutionary action: their object is to secure palliations of the capitalist system, not to abolish it.

British experience has shown that the workers' council system is efficient both as an engine for fighting the employer, and as a means of administrating the industry. Experience has also shown that under favourable conditions it can be built up with remarkable rapidity.

Experience in those European countries where the workers and their organisations have been tested in the revolutionary fight, has shown that the workers' council is always the organ of the workers' struggle. The Trade Unions, having tried unsuccessfully to avert the contest, in each case threw the weight of their influence on to the side of preserving the established order, and opposed every effort of the workers and their councils to overpower the employing class.

The evidence given by J.H. Thomas in his libel case against the Communist and its officials reveals the attitude which he will adopt in the event of any struggles for Proletarian power in this country. J.H. Thomas must not be regarded as an exception: the British Trade Union officials will all adopt the same attitude. Some will denounce the revolutionary workers on platforms, openly proclaiming their allegiance to the Crown, the Government and the employing class; others will merely hold aloof from the revolutionaries and in the Trade Union conferences will vote against the Unions joining the revolutionaries in the struggle. If they do not advise Trade Union members to give actual assistance to the Government in coercing the revolutionaries, they will at least advise their members to assist the cause of re-establishing the disturbed capitalist order by remaining quietly at work — the obedient servants of the capitalist employer, or of the capitalist Government.

This is the part which the Trade Unions and their officials have played in every one of the many recent proletarian uprisings in other countries: this is the part which J.H. Thomas and his colleagues will play here. J.H. Thomas differs only in degree from his colleagues who belong to the Reformist School. The British Trade Union movement and its officials belong to the same school as the Trade Unions and Trade Union officials of Europe and America.

The Trade Unions have too loose and uncoordinated a structure to make the revolution: they are ideologically opposed to it: therefore they will fight it.

The workers' councils, co-ordinated industrially and nationally along the lines of production and distribution, are the organs which are structurally fitted to give the workers greatest power in the control of industry. If that power is to be used to overthrow the present system, the councils, which together will form a "One Big Union" of workers' committees in all industries, should be built, from the first, with the object of taking control.

In Germany, where the methods necessary for waging the proletarian struggle are being forged during the struggle, the Revolutionary Workers' Union, the A.A.U., is a fighting force which has had to be reckoned with. Its growth has been accelerated by the fact that the reactionary Trade Unions have expelled their revolutionary members.

Part Seven
Workers Dreadnought March 11th 1922

The great task of the Communist revolution is ideologic. Communism entails the creation of an altogether new attitude of mind towards all social relationships, and the development of a host of new habits and impulses. In discarding our purse and our financial anxieties and calculations, in removing the dependence of the propertiless upon the propertied, we shall change the entire configuration of life. Communism will create for us a great fraternity, a great trustfulness, arising from a great security, an abundant enthusiasm for productive labour, because such labour will benefit all, and all will share responsibility for it.

Communism necessitates the creation of a great initiative, which shall animate the entire people.

Under Capitalism the masses are as a flock of sheep driven by their owners. Under Communism, on the contrary, they will be free co-operators, producing, inventing, studying, not under the compulsion of law, or poverty, or the incentive of individual gain, but from deliberate choice and with an eager zest for achievement. Communism will provide the material and spiritual conditions which will make voluntary co-operative labour possible. Only by willing service and intelligent initiative can true Communism develop.

The establishment of the Communist life entails a complete breach, both in practice and in ideas, with Capitalism and its machinery. The Parliamentary system is the characteristic machinery of the capitalist State; it has grown up with great similarity in all the countries which have built up their own capitalism. In countries where an alien Capitalism dominates the native populace, the Parliamentary system of the dominant aliens extends the tentacles of its power to the subject country. It sends its officials overseas to rule the natives, entirely discarding its pretended dependence on the consent of the governed and its boasted representative character.

Parliament has been in large measure the co-operative society of the landlords and capitalists through which they have policed the proletariat at home and maintained their power abroad.

The great landlords originally used lawless force and violence for seizing their estates. In the latter half of the fifteenth century they, as feudal lords, drove the peasants, who had the same feudal right to the land as they, from their holdings. The feudal lords usurped the lands which were held and used in common. These things they did in defiance of law and custom, and without waiting to obtain the assent or assistance of Parliament.

Later on, however, the feudal lords found it convenient to give Parliamentary sanction to their robbery of the peasants, and to enact legislation to complete their usurpation of the land. Sitting in Parliament, the lords proceeded thereafter to abolish their own merely feudal tenure of the land, and by creating the modern right of private property in land, they made themselves its absolute owners.

Before they had legalised the expropriation of the peasants, the lords in Parliament enacted legislation to force the peasants they were driving from the land to become their wage-slaves. From the reign of Henry VII, legislation began for the coercion of the dispossessed. We all know that for begging, or wandering without means of subsistence, the landless people were whipped and branded, their ears were sliced, and on a third arrest they were executed. An Act of Edward VI condemned the idler to be the slave of whoever denounced him. He could be sold, bequeathed, or hired as a slave. Any-one might make slaves of his children. Vagabonds, as the dispossessed were called, might be made into parish slaves, condemned to labour for the inhabitants. Only in the reign of Anne, when an industrial proletariat sufficient for the needs of farmers and manufacturers had been developed, were such statutes repealed. So long ago as 1349, Parliament, in the Statute of Labourers, fixed maximum wages to prevent the proletariat from asserting itself to the inconvenience of the employing classes. Maximum wage legislation was maintained thereafter as long as any serious tendency to labour scarcity could give the workers a powerful lever in forcing up their wages.

Parliament has remained the employers' co-operative society for dragooning the workers, in spite of all the extensions of the franchise which have taken place. When a serious labour scarcity arose in our time, during the great European war of 1914-19, Parliament enacted the Munitions Act, to prevent the workers taking advantage of the situation.

Neither in this present period of great unemployment, nor at any other time in history, has Parliament fixed maximum wages to protect the workers when the employers have been taking advantage of a Labour surplus to depress the wages of their employees below the subsistence level. The rates of wages fixed by the Agricultural Wages Boards during the war, were, in reality, a method of attaining by subtle means, the object which the Munitions Act achieved in other industries: namely a check on the bargaining power of Labour during a period of unexampled labour scarcity.

From the early laws against the industrial combination of the workers (maintained by the coercive power of the state as long as the ruling classes considered them necessary) down to our modern D.O.R.A. and E.P.A. and the strike-breaking machinery employed by the government in the last railway and mining strikes, Parliamentary Government has never failed to protect the possessions of the landlords and capitalists, and to employ whatever coercive measures have been necessary to provide the landlords and capitalists with disciplined workers.

Parliament and its accessories have been fashioned by the ruling classes for their service. The Courts of Law are strongholds of tradition and privilege, and appointment to the judicial Bench is made obscurely and arbitrarily by the Government.

In case of dispute, the Government-appointed irremovable judges interpret the Parliament-made law. The Government-hired prosecutor — who may even be a member of the Government, is leagued with the Government-appointed judge against the accused. All the force of the Government police assists the prosecution. In political trials, acquittals are remarkably rare. The judges, drawn from the privileged class, almost invariably decide against the popular cause.

The local governing bodies have no power to legislate or initiate: they merely administer the Acts of Parliament under the cramping supervision of Government Departments, which make rules interpreting the Acts of Parliament. Either with, or without Parliamentary sanction, Government departments determine what the local authorities shall spend, by limiting their power to levy Rates and to contract loans, and by prohibiting them from trading, except by special permission of the Government.

As to Parliament itself, its powers have been almost all annexed by the Cabinet.

The King, who is supposed to obey the Government, decides when Parliament shall assemble. The Government decides what subjects Parliament shall discuss, and on what it shall legislate. The Government drafts the legislation. If a measure be amended in a manner displeasing to the Government, the Government withdraws the measure, and either drops it altogether, or re-introduces it in another form. Parliament cannot proceed with any measure unless the Government desire it.

The Speaker and Chairman of Committee appointed by the Government, control the debate and interpret the rules of procedure. Parliamentary discipline is exceedingly strict. No one may speak until called upon by the Speaker, or Chairman of Committee, and the Speaker, or Chairman, may stop any speech, and even prevent the asking of a question, on the ground, either that it is out of order or "it is not in the public interest" that a reply be given. There is no appeal from the ruling of the Chair, which is enforced by the officials of the House, who at once eject any Member failing to obey the Chair.

The Government must have a majority in the House of Commons, or it cannot remain in power. That majority is composed of Party hacks with no chance of being returned to Parliament, except by the aid of the Party machinery and funds. They will not vote against the Government, because to do so would be to incur the ostracism of the Party leaders, and consequently of the Party; such ostracism would inevitably mean the loss of their Parliamentary seats at the next election. The Party man who disobeys his Party must either retire from politics, or become a candidate of the opposite Party (if it will have him, which may not be the case). Many years have passed since a Government was turned out by a hostile Parliamentary vote of its supporters. Even its political opponents are apt to shrink from defeating a Government on a critical issue, which would mean its resignation, for that in most cases entails a General Election. A General Election is of all things that which is most detested by the average Member of Parliament. It means for him an election campaign of tremendous exertion, in which he is compelled to speak at an extraordinary number of meetings, besides canvassing voters and calling on people of influence. Moreover, he may lose his seat, and thus suffer the defeat of many of his ambitions, as well as the loss of an income of four hundred pounds a year. The Member of Parliament prepared to take a line independent of his Party on any subject of importance is exceedingly rare. He is soon eliminated from Parliament.

The Prime Minister is chosen by the Sovereign from amongst the most prominent leaders of the Party which gains the majority of the Parliamentary seats in the General Election. Persons of powerful influence, of course, make representations to the Sovereign, and the Party caucus and its rival big-wigs all put in their word. What private understandings and guarantees are exacted the people do not know. The Sovereign appoints the rest of the Cabinet on the advice of the Prime Minister, who is influenced, of course, by the powerful personages who provide Party funds, who control Party newspapers, and who are powerful in banking and other circles able to sabotage the Government activities. The wire-pulling and intrigue that surround the making of Cabinets have only been slightly revealed in the memoirs of some of the privileged few who have been behind the scenes.

The policies of Government Departments are supposed to be controlled in general outline by the Cabinet as a whole, and in fuller detail by the Minister at the head of each Department who is appointed by the Prime Minister. The Departments are vast and deal with vast work; the Cabinet of party hacks and political adventurers knows little of the Departments. The responsible Minister, who usually remains in a particular Department no more than a year or two at most, and often no more than a few months, rarely learns much about his work; the permanent officials are the real masters of the administrative detail, and their policy is broadly that of the prevailing capitalist opinion current at the time. Lavish extravagance on Departmental expenditure, and ruthless parsimony towards the people, the great unofficial, unprivileged masses, who are treated as tiresome mendicants, is the outstanding characteristic of administration by Government Departments.

Members of Parliament know little of the doings of Government Departments. The debates, held twice or thrice a year, and the questions, to which cursory answers are given and on which no discussion is permitted, are the only opportunities by which Members may acquire information. Ministers in charge of Departments report once or twice a year what they choose of what their Departments have done.

Members of Parliament may move to reduce the amount Parliament is to vote for the Department in question, as a protest against something that displeases them, or as a matter of political form. Such motions are usually defeated or withdrawn. If, however such a motion be carried, the Government may resign, if the question involved be important. Generally, in such rare cases, the Government brings the vote up again another day, and, by rallying its supporters, it defeats the motion. Perhaps as a result of the incident the Minister whose Department has been criticised, moves on to another Department. His old place is taken by one whose policy differs but little from his own.

The House of Commons has no effective check on the doings of the Cabinet: it knows very little of what the Cabinet is actually about; the Press is given more information on questions of State than are the ordinary Members of Parliament.

The House of Lords, with its hereditary members, can check and thwart the doings of the Government more effectively than can the House of Commons, although its power is specifically limited. Its Members are not dependent on the machinery of the Party to secure their election. Their Parliamentary seats are theirs for life: no-one can dislodge them. The older Lords, at least, are probably no longer seeking the favour of Party leaders and Members of the Government to assist their personal fortunes. Though, perhaps, less open to personal corruption than the ambitious political hacks of the House of Commons, the Members of the House of Lords are, of course, even more surely lined up as one man against the emancipation of the proletariat and in defence of the present system.

In all this the electors are remote outsiders. They have no hold on the Members of the House of Commons who are supposed to represent them. They must decide for which candidate to vote on the general programme of the Party promoting the candidature, for, if returned, the Member will have no power except through his Party. No item of the Party programme is binding, no pledge given by the candidate or his Party can be relied on. The programme is enunciated during the election in vaguely-worded speeches and manifestos, every point in which will probably be discarded. Not until the next election will the voter have another chance to pass judgement on the actions of the candidate who won the seat in his local constituency, or on those of the Government in power. The Member, meanwhile, has probably been merely a cipher in Parliament; the Government has done nothing pleasing to the elector; but the opposing Party, in the vague compound of catch-cries called its programme, offers nothing that promises satisfaction. The constituency is vast: the electors have no personal knowledge of either candidate. The election is decided by such questions as which Party machine has most systematically traced the absent voters and made the best arrangements to bring them to the poll, which Party has the most motor cars lent to it for taking voters on free rides to the polling booth, which Party is served by the local paper having the largest circulation in the district.

Even were it possible to democratise the machinery of Parliament, its inherently anti-Communist character would still remain. The King might be replaced by a President, or all trace of the office abolished. The House of Lords might disappear, or be transformed into a Senate. The Prime Minister might be chosen by a majority vote of Parliament, or elected by referendum of the people. The Cabinet might be chosen by referendum, or become an Executive Committee elected by Parliament. The doings of Parliament might be checked by referendum.

Nevertheless, Parliament would still be a non-Communist institution. Under Communism we shall have no such machinery of legislation and coercion. The business of the Soviets will be to organise the production and supply of the common services; they can have no other lasting function.

PART FOUR
Otto Rühle

The Revolution Is Not A Party Affair

(1920)

Parliamentarism appeared with the domination of the bourgeoisie. Political parties appeared with parliament.

In parliaments the bourgeois epoch found the historical arena of its first contentions with the crown and nobility. It organised itself politically and gave legislation a form corresponding to the needs of capitalism. But capitalism is not something homogeneous. The various strata and interest groups within the bourgeoisie each developed demands with differing natures. In order to bring these demands to a successful conclusion, the parties were created which sent their representatives and activists to the parliaments. Parliament became a forum, a place for all the struggles for economic and political power, at first for legislative power but then, within the framework of the parliamentary system, for governmental power. But the parliamentary struggles as struggles between parties, are only battles of words. Programmes, journalistic polemics, tracts, meeting reports, resolutions, parliamentary debates, decisions nothing but words. Parliament degenerated into a talking shop (increasingly as time passed). But from the start parties were only mere machines for preparing for elections. It was no chance that they originally were called "electoral associations".

The bourgeoisie, parliamentarism, and political parties mutually and reciprocally conditioned one another. Each is necessary for the others. None is conceivable without the others. They mark the political physiognomy of the bourgeois system, of the bourgeois-capitalist system.

The revolution of 1848 was still-born. But the democratic state, the ideal of the bourgeois era was erected. The bourgeoisie, impotent and faint-hearted by nature provided no force and displayed no will to realise this ideal in the struggle. It knuckled under to the crown and the nobility, contenting itself with the right to exploit the masses economically and so reducing parliamentarism to a parody.

So resulted the need for the working class to send representatives to parliament. These then took the democratic demands out of the perfidious hands of the bourgeoisie. They carried out energetic propaganda for them. They tried to inscribe them in legislation. Social-Democracy adopted a minimum democratic programme to this end: a programme of immediate and practical demands adapted to the bourgeois period. Its parliamentary activity was dominated by this programme. It was also dominated by a concern to gain the advantages of a legalised field of manoeuvre both for the working class and its own political activity, through the construction and perfection of a liberal-bourgeois formal democracy.

When Wilhelm Liebknecht proposed a refusal to take up parliamentary seats, it was a matter of failing to recognise the historical situation. If Social-Democracy wanted to be effective as a political party, it would have to enter parliament. There was no other way to act and to develop politically.

When the syndicalists turned away from parliamentarism and preached anti-parliamentarism, this did honour to their appreciation of the growing emptiness and corruption of parliamentary practice. But in practice, they demanded something impossible of Social-Democracy: that it take a position contrary to the historical situation and renounce itself. It could not take up this view. As a political party it had to enter parliament.

The KPD has also become a political party, a party in the historical sense, like the German Social Democratic Party (SPD) and the Independent Social-Democrats (USPD).

The leaders have the first say. They speak, they promise, they seduce, they command. The masses, when they are there, find themselves faced with a fait-accompli. They have to form up in ranks and march in step. They have to believe, to be silent, and pay up. They have to receive their orders and carry them out. And they have to vote.

Their leaders want to enter parliament. They have to elect them. Then while the masses abide by silent obedience and devoted passivity, the leaders decide the policy in parliament.

The KPD has become a political party. It also wants to enter parliament. It lies when it tells the masses that it only wants to enter parliament in order to destroy it. It lies when it states that it does not want to carry out any positive work in parliament. It will not destroy parliament; it doesn't want to and it can't. It will do "positive work" in parliament, it is forced to, it wants to. This is its life.

The KPD has become a parliamentary party like any other; a party of compromise, opportunism, criticism and verbal jousting a party that has ceased to be revolutionary.

Consider this:

It entered parliament. It recognised the trade unions. It bowed before the democratic constitution. It makes peace with the ruling powers. It places itself on the terrain of real force relations. It takes part in the work of national and capitalist reconstruction.

How is it different from the USPD? It criticises instead of repudiating. It acts as the opposition instead of making the revolution. It bargains instead of acting. It chatters away instead of struggling. That is why it had ceased to be a revolutionary organisation.

It has become a Social-Democratic party. Only a few nuances distinguish it from the Scheidemanns (SPD) and the Daumigs(USPD). This is how it has finished up.

The masses have one consolation; there is an opposition. But this opposition has not broken away from the counter-revolution.

What could it do? What has it done? It has assembled and united a political organisation. Was this necessary?

From a revolutionary point of view the most decisive and active elements, the most mature elements have to form themselves into a phalanx of the revolution. They can only do this through a firm and solid foundation. They are the elite of the new revolutionary proletariat. By the firm character of their organisation they gain in strength and their judgment develops a greater profundity. They demonstrate themselves as the vanguard of the proletariat, as an active will in relation to hesitant and confused individuals. At decisive moments they form a magnetic centre of all activity. They are a political organisation but not a political party, not a party in the traditional sense.

The title of the Communist Workers Party (KAPD) is the last external vestige – soon superfluous – of a tradition that can't be simply wiped away when the living mass ideology of yesterday no longer has any relevance. But this last vestige will also be removed.

The organisation of communists in the front line of the revolution must not be the usual sort of party, on pain of death, on pain of following the course of the KPD.

The epoch of the foundation of parties is over, because the epoch of political parties in general is over. The KPD is the last party. Its bankruptcy is the most shameful, its end is without dignity or glory. . . .But what comes of the opposition? of the revolution?

The revolution is not a party affair. The three social-democratic parties (SPD, USPD, KPD) are so foolish as to consider the revolution as their own party affair and to proclaim the victory of the revolution as their party goal. The revolution is the political and economic affair of the totality of the proletarian class. Only the proletariat as a class can lead the revolution to victory. Everything else is superstition, demagogy and political chicanery. The proletariat must be conceived of as a class and its activity for the revolutionary struggle unleashed on the broadest possible basis and in the most extensive framework.

This is why all proletarians ready for revolutionary combat must be got together at the workplace in revolutionary factory organisations, regardless of their political origins or the basis by which they are recruited. Such groups should be united in the framework of the General Workers Union (AAU).

The AAU is not indiscriminate, it is not a hotchpotch nor a chance amalgam. It is a regroupment for all proletarian elements ready for revolutionary activity, who declare themselves for class struggle, the council system and the dictatorship of the proletariat. It is the revolutionary army of the proletariat.

This General Workers Union is taking root in the factories, building itself up in branches of industry from the base up federally at the base, and through revolutionary shop-stewards at the top. It exerts pressure from the base up, from the working masses. It is built according to their needs; it is the flesh and blood of the proletariat; the force that motivates it is the action of the masses; its soul is the burning breath of the revolution. It is not the creation of some leaders, it is not a subtly altered construction. It is neither a political party with parliamentary chatter and paid hacks, nor a trade union. It is the revolutionary proletariat.

So what will the KAPD do?

It will create revolutionary factory organisations. It will propagate the General Workers Union. Factory by factory, industry by industry it will organise the revolutionary masses. They will be prepared for the onslaught, given the power for decisive combat, until the last resistance offered by capitalism as it collapses is overcome.

It will inspire the fighting masses with confidence in their own strength, the guarantee for victory in that confidence will free them ambitious and traitorous leaders.

From this General Workers Union the communist movement will emerge, starting in the factories, then spreading itself over economic regions and finally over the entire country, i.e. a new communist "party" which is no longer a party, but which is, for the time communist! The heart and head of the revolution!

We shall show this process in a concrete way:

There are 200 men in a factory. Some of them belong to the AAU and agitate for it, at first without success. But during the first struggle the trade unions naturally give in and the old bonds are broken. Some 100 men have gone over to the AAU. Amongst them there are 20 communists, the others being from the USPD, syndicalists and unorganised. At the beginning the USPD inspires most confidence. Its politics dominate the tactics of the struggles carried out in the factory. However slowly but surely, the politics of the USPD are proved false, non-revolutionary. The confidence that the workers have in the USPD decreases. The politics of the communists are confirmed. The 20 communists become 50 then 100 and more. Soon the communist group politically dominates the whole of the factory, determining the tactics of the AAU, at the front of the revolutionary struggle. This is so both at the small scale and large scale. Communist politics take root from factory to factory, from economic region to economic region. They are realised, gaining command becoming both body and head, the guiding principle.

It is from such communist groups in the factories, from mass sections of communists in the economic regions that the new communist movement through the council system will come into being. As for "revolutionising" the trade unions or "restructuring" them. How long will that take? A few years? A few dozen years? Until 1926 perhaps. Anyway, the aim could not be to wipe out the clay giant of the trade unions with their 7 million members in order to reconstruct them in another form.

The aim is to seize hold of the commanding levers of industry for the process of social production and so to decisively carry the day in revolutionary combat, to seize hold of the lever that will let the air out of the capitalist system in entire industrial regions and branches.

It is here, in a mature situation, that the resolute action of a single organisation can completely surpass a general strike in effectiveness. It is here that the David of the factory can defeat the Goliath of the union bureaucracy.

The KPD has ceased to be the incarnation of the communist movement in Germany. Despite its noisy claims about Marx, Lenin and Radek it only forms the latest member of the counter)revolutionary united front. Soon it will present itself as the amiable companion of the SPD and USPD in the framework of a purely "socialist" workers government. Its assurance of being a "loyal" opposition to the murderous parties who have betrayed the workers is the first step. To renounce the revolutionary extermination of the Eberts and the Kautskys is already to tacitly ally oneself with them.

Ebert – Kautsky – Levi. The final stage of capitalism reaches its end, the last political relief of the German bourgeoisie the end.

The end also of parties, the politics of the parties, the deceit and treachery of the parties.

It is a new beginning for the communist movement the communist workers party, the revolutionary factory organisations regrouped in the General Workers Union, the revolutionary councils, the congress of revolutionary councils, the government of the revolutionary councils, the communist dictatorship of the councils.

Report from Moscow

(1920)

I travelled illegally to Russia. The business was difficult and dangerous; but it succeeded. On 16th June I stepped on to Russian soil: on the 19th I was in Moscow.

The departure from Germany went hastily. In April, upon invitation from Moscow, the KAPD (Communist Workers Party — Germany) had sent two comrades as negotiators to the Executive, to advise upon the KAPD's joining of the Third International. It was being said that the two comrades had been arrested in Estonia on the return journey. The necessity was to immediately recommence the negotiations and to bring them to completion and if possible to send back a report to the KAPD, so that information from the KAPD could be received before the start of the Congress.

All in the greatest rush, in that the congress should already begin on 15th June.

Having arrived in Russia, I found out to my joy that the news about the arrests of our comrades had been incorrect. They had travelled back via Murmansk and so were already in Norway on the way to Germany. I also learnt that the congress was not to begin on the 15th June but only on the 15th July.

What I further constituted was less pleasing. My first conversation with Radek was a real argument. Hours long. Partly highly vehement. Every sentence of Radek was a sentence out of the "Red Flag." Every argument a Spartacist argument. Radek is after all, lord and master of the KAPD. Dr. Levi and consorts are his willing parrots. They have no opinions of their own and are paid by Moscow.

I asked Radek to hand over to me the Open Letter to the KAPD. He promised me it, but didn't keep his word. I reminded him of it repeatedly still and others to remind him but didn't receive it. When I later heard that the two comrades who'd been acting as negotiators had only received the Open Letter only at the very last moment before their departure, the psychology of Radek's behaviour became clear to me. He, the wiliest of the wily, and the most unscrupulous of the unscrupulous, considering the perfidious lies and insolences which absolutely abounded in the Open Letter, felt of course something so like shame that he shied away from having to account for himself eye to eye with the insulted and libelled.

The methods which I saw practised on me in Moscow aroused my strongest aversions. Whereto I saw: political 'scene-shifting', calculated as bluff, using flashy revolutionary resolutions to conceal the opportunistic background. Best of all I'd have gone up and away again. However I decided to stay until the second delegate Comrade Merges-Braunschweig, would arrive.

I used the time to make studies.

First I looked around Moscow, mostly without official guidance, so as to also see that which wasn't decreed to be for viewing. Then I made a long car tour to Kashira and a trip to Nischny-Novgorod, Kasan Simbirsk, Samara, Saratov, Tambov, Tula, etc., thus getting to know the most important places in Central Russia. That provided an abundance of impressions more unpleasant than pleasant. Russia was suffering in all of its limbs, from every disease. But how could it have been any different! Lots was being reported but the example of Crispien and Dittman didn't tempt me to follow suit. Whose interests would be served then? Only the opponents of Communism. All these shortcomings and drawbacks aren't, of course, any evidence against Communism. At the most against the methods and tactics employed by Russia to realise Communism.

The Russian tactic is the tactic of authoritarian organisation. It has been so consistently developed and in the end carried to extremes, by the Bolsheviks to the fundamental principle of centralism that it has led to over-centralism. The Bolsheviks didn't do that out of wantonness or desire to experiment. The revolution forced them to it. If today the representatives of German party organisations are filled with indignation and cross themselves over the dictatorial and terroristic phenomena in Russia, its easy for them to talk. Were they in the position of the Russian government, they'd have to act exactly so.

Centralism is the organisational principle of the bourgeois-capitalist age. With it the bourgeois state and the capitalist economy can be built up. Not however the proletarian state and the socialist economy. They demand the council system. For the KAPD—contrary to Moscow—the revolution is no party matter, the party no authoritarian organisation from the top down, the leader no military chief, the masses no army condemned to blind obedience, the dictatorship no despotism of a ruling clique; communism no springboard for the rise of a new Soviet bourgeoisie. For the KAPD the revolution is the business of the whole proletarian class within which the communist party forms only the most mature and determined vanguard. The rise and development of the masses to political maturity of this vanguard doesn't await the tutelage of the leadership, discipline and regulation. On the contrary: these methods produce in an advanced proletariat such as the German exactly the opposite result. They strangle initiatives, paralyse the revolutionary activity, impair the combativeness, reduce the personal feeling of responsibility. What counts is to trigger the initiative of the masses, to free them from authority, to develop their self-confidence, to train them in self-activity and thereby to raise their interest in the revolution. Every fighter must know and feel why he is fighting, what he is fighting for. Everyone must become in his consciousness a living bearer of the revolutionary struggle and creative member of the communist build-up. The necessary freedom therefore will however never be won in the coercive system of centralism, the chains of bureaucratic-militaristic control, under the burden of a leader-dictatorship and its inevitable accompaniments: arbitrariness, personality cult, authority, corruption, violence. Therefore transformation of the party-conception into a federative community-conception on the line of councilist ideas. Therefore: supercession of external commitments and compulsion through internal readiness and willingness. Therefore: elevation of communism from the demagogic prattle of the paper cliché to the height of one of the most internally captivating and fulfilling experiences of the whole world.

The KAPD came to these of its conclusions through the simple realisation of the very obvious circumstance, that every country and every people because they have their own particular economy, social structure, traditions, maturity of the proletariat, i.e., their own particular revolutionary requirements and conditions, must also have their own revolutionary laws, methods, rhythm of development and outward appearances. Russia isn't Germany, Russian politics aren't German politics, Russian revolution isn't German revolution. Lenin might demonstrate hundreds of times that the tactics of the Bolsheviks were a brilliant success in the Russian Revolution — they wouldn't by a long way be the right tactics for the German revolution. Every attempt to force us to adopt these tactics must provoke the most decisive opposition.

Moscow is making this terroristic attempt. It wants to elevate its principles to the principles of world revolution. The KAPD is its agent. It works on Russian orders and to the Russian model. It is Moscow's gramophone. Because the KAPD doesn't play along in this eunuch-role, it is persecuted with deadly hate. One reads only the most insulting aspersions, the poisonous libels and accusations with which one fights us without hindsight of the revolutionary situation in which we stand and of the effect which this vile practice triggers in our bourgeois opponents. Dr. Levi and Heckert must fling at us every piece of rubbish that Radek and Zinoviev press into their hands. That's what those boys are paid for. However because the KAPD doesn't give in nevertheless it ought to be censured by the Congress of the III International to comply to Moscow's power-of-command. It was all excellently prepared. The guillotine was set up. Radek smugly tested the sharpness of the blade. And already the high court was sitting. It should have been a grand scene, too beautiful to be accomplished.

As I returned from the Volga, Comrade Merges had arrived in Moscow.

On the same day a sitting of the Executive of the III International took place. We weren't invited. In our absence, the motion of Meyer (KPD) that we should be refused admission to the Congress was discussed. The motion was rejected. On this they called us to the sitting, and were so gracious as to grant us advisory status at the Congress.

At this meeting we got to see the discussion guidelines which were to be laid before the Congress. They were intended to be the basis for the decisions of the Congress. Of which in his boastful manner Radek had already said to me earlier, that he had it in the pocket. "In the pocket!"

The discussion guidelines — weren't these not old familiars? Indeed. We recognised in them the notorious Heidelberg theses repeated. They were only somewhat more elaborately set out, somewhat theoretically doctored, somewhat enhanced in "Centralist-dictatorial". They were made into theses of Russian power-politics out of theses of Spartacist division-politics, and should now become theses of international violation by Russian methods.

We sacrificed a night to their study, and knew in the morning what we had to do.

We went to Radek, and put to him the question of if in the Open Letter (which still hadn't been given to us) the demanded expulsions of Laufenberg, Wolfheim and Rühle was an ultimatum, and if the Executive insisted upon the fulfilment of these demands before the KAPD would be admitted to the III International. Radek tried miscellaneous evasions, but we demanded a plain answer. Then Radek explained: It would satisfy the Executive if the KAPD promised that they would — at a later date, at a suitable opportunity — free themselves of Laufenberg and Wolfheim. Of my expulsion there wasn't any more question. This remarkable yielding to demands which had been raised with the truest ring of conviction as conditio sine qua non made us suspicious. Now we demanded to know which demands of the Executive concerning the admission of the KAPD into the III International were definitive. Radek explained: You must in the name of your party at the beginning of the Congress give the declaration that the KAPD will abide by all decision — then you'll receive voting status at Congress: then nothing will stand in the way of your admission into the III International.

Were we hearing right: in advance most solemnly declare that we wished to submit to the Congress decisions, which we didn't even know. . . .Was that supposed to be one of Radek's jokes?

No — it was serious.

Now if the Congress were to decide upon the dissolution of the KAPD?. . . . Joking apart: he did indeed have that intention.

Thereby Radek was unmasked.

What was in the theses then?

Ah now.

1. The communists are duty-bound to set themselves up in a rigid centralist, iron-hard, militaristic, dictatorial organisation.

2. The communists are duty-bound to take part in parliamentary elections, and to enter parliament to carry out a new type of revolutionary parliamentary work there.

3. The communists are duty-bound to remain in the trade unions so as to help the revolution to victory in these revolutionarily-transformable institutions.

4. Each of the parties that are members of the III International is to call itself the Communist Party, consequently the KAPD has to sacrifice its continuing independence and dissolve itself into the KPD.

Thus joking apart: the Congress actually should pronounce the death sentence upon the KAPD, and we, the KAPD delegates, should receive voting status, i.e. we should be able to help pronounce the death sentence, if we were to declare prior that the KAPD wanted to submit to the pronounced death sentence without resistance.

Could there be a greater political comedy? Or a greater perfidy?

We laughed in Radek's face, and asked if he was mad.

A party, that on the grounds of the Heidelberg theses had split from the KPD, had constituted itself on a new basis, and had given itself organisationally a new structure, tactically a new orientation and theoretically a new programme, that vigorously stood on its own two feet, concentrated in itself all the active forces of the German revolution and in size of membership is far superior to the KPD — such a party refuses, may, indeed must refuse, even once to enter into a discussion on the discussion of its right to exist. As a child can never return to its mother's womb, likewise the KAPD doesn't return to the KPD. Even one word of discussion about this is mischief, is absurdity, is a political childishness.

We left Radek standing so, with the hangman's rope that he had intended to put around the neck of the KAPD, and went on our way. We felt no desire to give ourselves further headaches in this atmosphere of political trickery and cheating, of diplomatic stage-management and opportunistic string-pulling, of lack of moral restraint and cold-grinning cunning.

Inside ourselves we had nothing, nothing at all to look for in a congress which met so far from all communism.

Therefore we declared: "We decline with thanks participation in the Congress. We have decided to travel home, to recommend to the KAPD a wait-and-see attitude, until a truly revolutionary International has come into being, which it can join. Adios!"

Our decision had a surprising effect. If until then we were treated like spoilt children, whose misdeeds caused the poor parents anxiety and vexation, and should be put across the knee and given a good hiding, so they now suddenly started to come round. The threateningly swung whip disappeared behind the mirror, and the carrot was brought out of the drawer. They began to woo us with brotherly words, such as should be customary between communists, and with the appearance of goodwill towards objective communication. Even Radek took on manners. He negotiated reasonably and railed against the KPD, who he called, "a lazy and cowardly gang", who he would make "wet their pants", etc. We had prolonged and thorough discussions with him, Zinoviev, Bucharin and at the last moment even a determined discussion with Lenin. The great respect and high admiration that we have for him, and that through this discussion were raised even further, did not prevent us telling him, in a totally German manner, our opinions. We explained to him that we felt it a scandal and a crime against the German revolution, that in a time when hundreds of brochures had to be written opposing opportunism, he found the time and felt occasioned to write a brochure exactly against the KAPD—the active and most consistent party of the German revolution, which now, like his other writings of recent times, was being used by the entire counter-revolution as an arsenal, not to correct our supposedly wrong tactic in the interest of the revolution, but to knock dead every stirring activity of the masses with arguments and quotes from Lenin. We demonstrated to him that he is completely misinformed about conditions in Germany, and that his arguments for the revolutionary exploitation of the parliament and the trades unions only have a laughable effect. We finally left him without the slightest doubt that the KAPD, as it refuses any material help from Moscow, also with complete determination won't stand for any interference from Moscow in its politics.

The discussions left in us the feeling that the Russian comrades had begun to appreciate what a mistake it had been to go too far. That in the end the International, i.e. in the first line Russia, needed the KAPD more than vice versa, the KAPD the International. So for them our decision was most unpleasant, and they sought a compromise. As we were in Petrograd on the way home, the Executive sent after us another invitation to the Congress with the statement that the KAPD (although it hadn't complied with or promised to comply with a single one of the draconian conditions of the Open Letter) had been allowed the right to the voting status at the Congress. Too crude a bait! Fundamentally it was of course a matter of complete indifference whether the KAPD assisted at its proposed execution in Moscow with advisory or voting status. So we gave our thanks once more and travelled to Germany.

The outcome of the Congress had justified our tactics. The decisions taken on the questions of concern to us – building of the party, parliamentarianism, trade union politics – reveal the most unconcealed opportunism. They are decisions on the line of the right wing of the USP, decisions that even to the interpretation of the Däumigs, Curt Geyers, Koenens, etc., on the parliamentary and trades unions questions mean a violation. But can and should the KAPD share the same Congress decisions on the same ground with the USP? One must answer in the affirmative to this question and think out the consequences in order to judge the complete monstrosity and absolute impossibility of the KAPD joining this III International.

This is not to say that we wished to oppose the organisational unification of communist workers and an international alliance of the revolutionary proletariat. By no means! We only mean, that the affiliation to an actual revolutionary International will not be decided through paper Congress decisions and the goodwill of the strata of the hierarchies. It decides itself through the will to struggle and the revolutionary activities of the masses in the hour of the decision. It is the product of the great purifying and maturing processes of the revolution, which eliminates everything halfway and wrong and only lets the true and whole count. The KAPD may confidently look forward to this decision, then it will rise to the historic task that awaits it.

As I said good-bye to Lenin, I said to him: "Hopefully the next Congress of the Third International can take place in Germany. Then we will have brought you the concrete evidence that we were in the right. Then you will have to correct your point of view." To which Lenin replied laughing: "If it so happens, then we would be the last to stand in the way of correction."

May it so happen! It will so happen!

Printed in the United States
104466LV00001B/72/A